796.332
CHA

W9-BCR-221

796.332   Champions on the field
CHA

WITHDRAWN
Fairhope Public Library

CHAMPIONS
ON THE FIELD

714590

FAIRHOPE PUBLIC LIBRARY
161 N. SECTION ST.
FAIRHOPE, AL 36532

JUN 0 1 2006

Copyright © 1993 *The Birmingham News*, Birmingham, Alabama.
All rights reserved.

We are pleased for excerpts from this book to be used in newspaper articles or reviews. Otherwise, no part of this publication may be reproduced, stored in a retrieval system or transmitted, in any form or by any means, electronic, mechanical, photocopying, recording or otherwise without the written permission of the publisher.

ISBN 0-9635413-2-3

Book Design and Layout: Lori Leath Smith

Printed by Ebsco Media
Birmingham, Alabama

Copies of this book may be obtained from:
The Birmingham News
Division of Special Projects
P.O. Box 2553
Birmingham, AL 35202
(205) 325-3188
Mail orders should include a check or money order for $11.50 per book.

TABLE OF CONTENTS

Steve Barnette photo

DEDICATION

To Pat Dye,
may the 1993 Tiger season
bring you lasting joy.

No one has enjoyed Auburn's success more than Dye

Neal Sims, News staff writer

AUBURN—The year has been harsh at times, gentle at times, but a year has passed since Pat Dye coached his last game at Auburn.

He wore a smile Tuesday and was chasing another, one that would come with an Auburn victory over Alabama Saturday.

"I'm sure there's somebody out there that wants to win this one worse than I do, but I don't know who it would be," Dye said Tuesday at the Auburn Alumni Center, where he works as special assistant to AU president William V. Muse.

That includes Terry Bowden, who took over for Dye and has taken the Tigers to a 10-0 mark and No. 6 national ranking in his first season. "Down deep," said Dye, "he hasn't enjoyed this a bit more than I have. I could smile from now until next year. Winning Saturday would put a lot of salve on some old wounds."

The old wounds include a tarnished final two seasons that tainted what otherwise was a glorious dozen years for Auburn football. Then charges by former player Eric Ramsey and his attorney Donald Watkins resulted in a two-

year NCAA investigation and sanctions against Auburn for providing extra benefits to Ramsey when he played for Dye.

Dye announced his resignation on the eve of last year's Auburn-Alabama game in Birmingham, and his team went out with a 17-0 loss, the only shutout of Dye's career.

"There are some people in this state that tried to destroy me and tried to destroy Auburn," said Dye. "They didn't succeed at either one. They are small enough and narrow-minded enough that they would be devastated by Auburn going 11-0. I'm not going to call any names. The ones who know who I'm talking about know who I'm talking about.

"The thing they didn't realize—that I've known for some time and Auburn people have known forever—is that this institution is stronger and has weathered more storms because that's the character of the school. When things are at their worst is when Auburn people stand the tallest. That's been very gratifying for me to witness."

The Tigers have gone undefeated, mostly with players recruited by Dye, and he's taken his satisfaction in that accomplishment.

"I've had fun every Saturday," he said. "That's about as good as you can do.

"They're not leading the league in offense. They're not leading the league in defense. They're just leading the league.

"I wouldn't have enjoyed this football season any more if I had been standing on the sidelines with them. I don't have any regrets whatsoever as far as not being able to go through this experience with them.

"If I had been the coach this year," added Dye, "we may be 7-3 or 6-4. Who knows? What we've got is a great situation at Auburn with the brightest young coach in the country. I'm excited about what he's done with this football team this year with kids I'm very close to and care about a great deal. I'm also excited about what he's going to do for Auburn in the future.

"Terry and his staff have done a great job. If I had to go back and coach next year, I'd be a better coach because I've learned some things watching Terry.

"I'll forever be indebted to Terry and his staff for the way I've been treated this year. They have let me be a part of this football team on my own terms," said Dye, who's made three trips on game days to be with his old team.

He came to the field before the season-opener with Ole Miss and before the homecoming game against New Mexico State. He was in the locker room after the Tigers captured national attention with their victory over Florida.

Saturday, Dye plans to make a personal visit again. He'll get up in the early hours, run his bird dogs and feed his cows on the farm, then sign his biography for two hours at a downtown bookstore.

When he makes it to Jordan-Hare Stadium, Dye said he will go down on the field and talk with both Alabama and Auburn coaches during pregame warmups. He'll watch the game from a skybox.

Afterward, Dye said, "There's something I would like Terry and the team to know when it is over with, and the outcome has no significance."

Coach Terry Bowden and players await the signal to charge onto the field for their final struggle of the season—against Alabama.

Joe Songer photo

FOREWORD

November 25, 1992: Pat Dye resigns.

November 26, 1992: Alabama beats Auburn for the third straight year, 17-0, Auburn finishes 5-5-1, NCAA probation looms.

In 100 years of Auburn football, one would be hard-pressed to remember more troubled times on the Plains.

But one year later .....

November 20, 1993: Auburn beats Alabama at Jordan-Hare Stadium, 22-14. The Tigers' magic-carpet ride through the 1993 season ends 11-0. Probation makes them ineligible for the Southeastern Conference championship and locks them out of a bowl. But they are champions on the field.

In 101 years of Auburn football, one would be hard-pressed to remember better times than these.

The 1993 Auburn Tigers righted the ship when it was sinking. When holes kept popping up in the dike, they plugged them up with their thumbs. They fed the multitudes with a loaf of bread and a fish.

A miracle?

That's a good word for it. Nobody thought they could do it, but this amazing team went undefeated, and even outdid the original Amazin's of 1972, who went 10-1 and blocked Alabama 17-16.

Not to forget Terry Henley, Randy Walls, Mike Neel, Rusty Deen, Mike Fuller, Ken Bernich, Bill Newton, David Langner, et al, from the story year of '72, when Auburn was picked to finish near the bottom of the SEC.

And not to forget that salty bunch of 1957 - Red Phillips, Lloyd Nix, Tommy Lorino, Bobby Hoppe, Billy Atkins, Zeke Smith, Cleve Wester, Jackie Burkett, Jerry Wilson, Tim Baker ... certainly not to forget Ralph "Shug" Jordan.

The '57 team won the national championship while on probation. But it was supposed to be good. Thirty-six years later, the '93 Auburn team entered the season with the odds stacked against it. What could you have gotten in Las Vegas that this team would go 11-0? They would have laughed into their hands, then quoted you 600 to 1.

Less than a month before the 1993 season began, Auburn learned of the terms of its probation after Eric Ramsey's allegations of payments from AU coaches. The university was sentenced to no bowl games for two seasons, no television for one.

To make matters worse, the Tigers were coming off a 5-5-1 season and the media were picking them to finish near the bottom of the SEC West Division.

But, after a three-week search for Pat Dye's successor, Auburn hitched its hopes on a 37-year-old coach with the bloodlines of a Triple Crown thoroughbred.

Terry Bowden, son of the famous Bobby Bowden, head coach at Florida State, moved up from Division I-AA Samford University to become the Tigers' new coach.

Bowden's boss at Samford, Dr. Thomas Corts, had warned Auburn people to "fasten their seatbelts" with Bowden in charge.

That was a good way to put it, because Bowden was a 5-foot-6, 160-pound ball of energy who quickly made his way around the state, speaking to civic clubs from Wedowee to Red Bay, getting to know Auburn fans and reassuring them that the program was in good hands.

Bowden was always available to the media, and he loved talking about Auburn football. Instead of the perfunctory few words that coaches normally give, he talked and talked and talked—so fast that reporters couldn't keep up with him in their notebooks.

He was secure enough to say in his introductory press conference that he would have to beat Alabama to really be accepted by Auburn people.

And he was good enough to do it in his first year.

What a year it was for Auburn and its fans.

In the following pages, *The Birmingham News* sports staff tells the story of Auburn's 1993 season, as it happened. This is the way the newspaper's sportswriters chronicled Bowden's first year, and the way the paper's photographers saw it through their lenses.

To Auburn fans everywhere, we sincerely hope you enjoy it.

—*Wayne Hester, News Sports Editor*

A joyous Wayne Gandy (74) and Anthony Harris (53) celebrate Auburn's victory over the Crimson Tide.

Bernard Troncale photo

Chapter One

11-0 Champions on the field

Terry Bowden: I finally feel like an Auburn man

Jimmy Bryan, News staff writer

AUBURN—The magic never left the Auburn Tigers. The tank full of miracles never ran dry.

The comebacks, the second-half heroics, the unlikely conclusions stayed with Auburn until the sweet end of 1993 here Saturday.

And this unbelievable season was topped off by the sweetest comeback of them all. Auburn turned an ugly first half into a 22-14 victory over Alabama before a soldout Jordan-Hare Stadium crowd of 85,214.

The Tigers (11-0 overall, 8-0 in the SEC) broke a three-game losing streak to Alabama (8-2-1, 5-2-1), finished the only 11-win season in the school's history and became one of only three undefeated, untied teams left in major college football. Nebraska and West Virginia are the other two.

Auburn's season is finished. NCAA probation denies the Tigers an SEC championship and bowl opportunity.

"This is the biggest win I've ever been part of," coach Terry Bowden said. "I've never been 11-0. This is the greatest thrill of my life. This is the only team in Auburn history to go 11-0.

"I can call this a great team now. With the emphasis on team. I finally feel like an Auburn man."

The Crimson Tide flashed to a 14-5 halftime lead and, like another team or two has done to Auburn this season, appeared to have the Tigers out of sorts.

Then Auburn turned the game around and shifted the momentum with one gutsy, unlikely

Auburn coaches intense on the sideline, searching for a winning combination.
Bernard Troncale photo

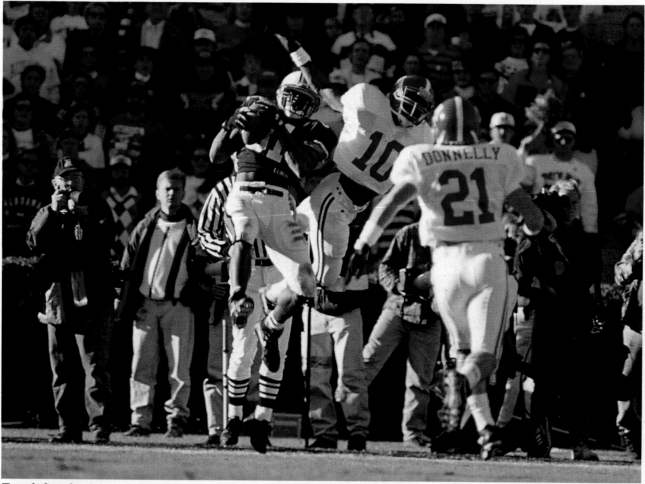

Frank Sanders' fourth-down touchdown catch over Alabama's Tommy Johnson sparked Auburn's comeback.
Joe Songer photo

play in the middle of the third quarter.

It was fourth-and-15 from the Alabama 35 after quarterback Stan White was slammed for a 6-yard loss by Jeremy Nunley and lost for the rest of the game (knee injury).

Coach Terry Bowden turned down a field goal, turned down a punt and sent backup Patrick Nix on for fourth down. Without benefit of a single warmup throw, Nix floated a 35-yard touchdown pass to Frank Sanders, and this game was never the same thereafter. The play was 78 Stay Z Takeoff. That's the technical name. It's a deep pattern to the short side of the field, the wide receiver faking short and taking off to the goal line. Sanders out-fought defensive back Tommy Johnson for the ball and leaped into the end zone.

"It was an interesting play," Bowden said. "It was a little too far for a field goal against the wind. I could just see a shanked punt, or one into the end

zone. That kind of pass is usually a touchdown or interception. We had nothing to lose."

Coach Gene Stallings saw it much the same way.

"I thought it was a good call and they executed it well," he said. "This was the big play that started them moving. I believe we were still in charge of the game, but momentum was turning in their favor."

Said Nix, "I just threw the ball up and Frank made a great catch."

That left Alabama with a diminishing 14-12 lead with 6:09 left in the third quarter.

Then Auburn took its next possession to Scott Ethridge's 26-yard field goal with 14:14 left in the game. That put the Tigers up 15-14 and turned out to be the winning points.

The Tigers got another touchdown on James Bostick's 70-yard breakaway with 2:19 left.

It was a game of many big plays.

Nix's throw to Sanders for the touchdown.

Bostic's 70-yard run.

Alabama's Kevin Lee flying 63 yards on a reverse for a touchdown.

Auburn tackling Tide quarterback Jay Barker for a safety.

Alabama going for a fourth-and-1 at its 29-yard-line with 8:55 left. And missing it.

"If I had it to do over, I'd do the same play," Stallings said. "I believed we could make it and if we didn't I thought we could hold them to a field goal."

Auburn marched to the 1-yard line, but botched the snap from center on a fourth down field goal attempt.

Alabama was crippled by a dozen penalties, most at killing times. The Tide was caught 12 times for 117 yards. Auburn was penalized four times for 37.

"Every time we did something we got penalized," Stallings said. "Penalties really hurt us. I feel bad about that. I really do."

Auburn's first points were a result of a penalty for illegal substitution (12 men on the field). Ethridge had missed a 52-yard field goal, but the 15-yard penalty gave Auburn new life. The Tigers marched to the 6-yard-line, and Ethridge kicked a 23-yarder on fourth down.

It was 3-0 with 1:48 left in the first quarter.

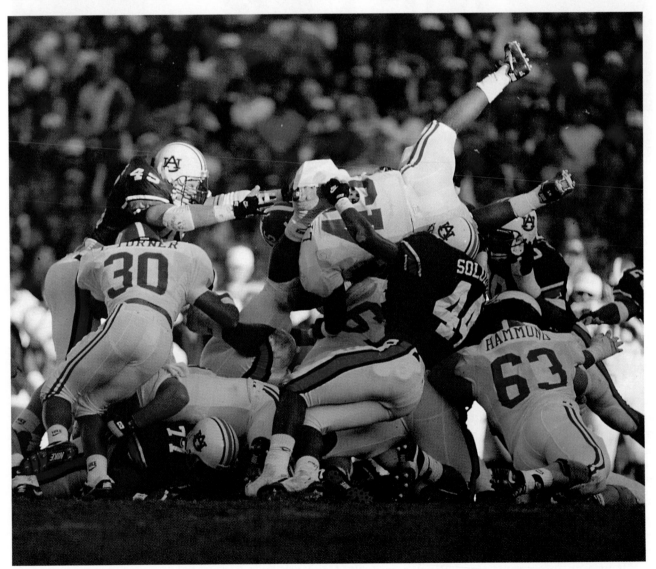

When Alabama's Tarrant Lynch tried for fourth-down heroics, the Auburn defense stuffed him on his own 29-yard-line deep in the fourth quarter.

Bernard Troncale photo

Alabama got the lead five minutes into the second. Starting from its 29, Bama scored in two plays—an 8-yard run by Chris Anderson and then Lee's 63-yard reverse.

Proctor's kick made it 7-3.

"We had a good offensive plan," Lee said. "It was just a matter of making the plays. That one went like you draw it up."

Next, Auburn's Jason Miska sacked Barker for a safety with 6:52 left in the half. It was 7-5.

Alabama scored just before the half, getting the ball at its 47 after a punt. Barker fired a 34-yard rocket to Lee at the Auburn 19. Anderson flashed into the end zone on the next play.

Proctor's kick made it 14-5 and that's the way they went to intermission.

Alabama had 193 yards of offense at the half, Auburn 125.

"Their defense just killed us in the first half," Bowden said.

"We performed well in the first half," Stallings said. "I thought we were in control of the game going into halftime." Alabama's offense was finished, however. Auburn's wasn't.

The dagger was Nix's off-the-bench pass to Sanders. With Ethridge's kick, Bama's lead was 14-12.

Then Auburn set out from its 40 and used 10 plays to reach the Bama 9-yard-line on fourth down. Ethridge kicked the Tigers into a 15-14 lead.

On the Tide's remaining possessions, Barker was intercepted, the Tide missed the fourth-and-1, Barker was intercepted again and fi-

Auburn's pounding tailback James Bostic found ample running room through the Bama defense including a 70-yard touchdown gallop.
Mark Almond photo

nally, time ran out.

Auburn had put another brilliant second half

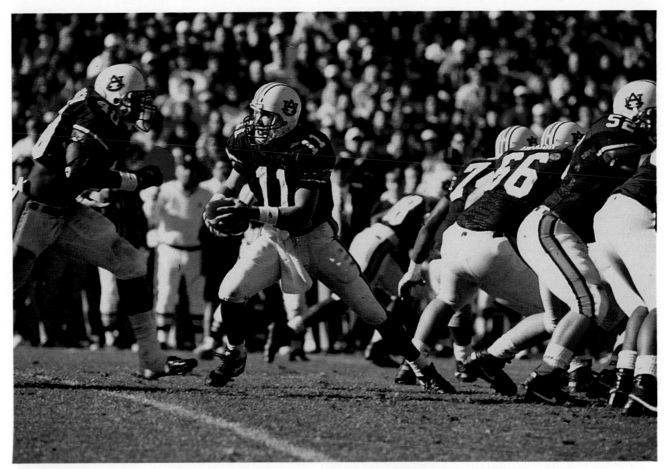

A solid Auburn offensive line holds out Bama defenders while quarterback Stan White and fullback Tony Richardson have time to operate.
Joe Songer photo

on the board. The Tigers finished with 351 yards to 269 for Alabama, 21 first downs to 10, 38:16 time of possession to 21:44.

And 22 points to 14.

This game too big? No way

Clyde Bolton, News columnist

AUBURN—Please, don't abuse me with that faddish remark that seems to be on the lips of so many who can't think of anything intelligent to say:

"The Auburn-Alabama game has become too big," they declare. "The teams shouldn't be annual opponents."

The Alabama-Auburn game is too big only if:

The Smoky Mountains are too big. Yellowstone is too big. A sunset on a clear autumn night is too big. The Statue of Liberty is too big. The Methodist Church is too big. A harvest moon is too big. The Pacific Ocean is too big.

The Auburn-Alabama game is this state at its zenith, and I don't apologize to anyone that it's "just a football game." I'll admit I don't care for opera, and I expect that many who say they do, don't either.

Two squads of young men who have worked harder in their young lives than you and I will ever work, who have disciplined themselves as you and I will never have to, who are regularly criticized by couch potatoes who couldn't tackle a dead corn-stalk, met on the floor of Jordan-Hare Stadium in the 58th Alabama-Auburn game Saturday, and I for one was pleased to live in the same state with them. They are among our best.

CLASSY PLAYERS

When, after the game, they lingered on the field to hug each other, Tiger and Tidesman, black and white, I thought the world could take a cue from these fellows. When Auburn quarterback Stan White was removed from the field with a leg injury and Alabama's players applauded him, I thought class often has a dirty face and a bloody nose.

Big? You bet the Auburn-Alabama game is big. Too big? Is the Mormon Tabernacle Choir too big? Is Mt. Rushmore too big? Too big is hundreds of soccer fans in Europe rioting. Too big isn't an Auburn fan sowing his neighbor's yard in winter rye grass that spells out 22 to 14.

Auburn's victory climaxed one of the great stories in the history of collegiate football. Terry Bowden, the minor leaguer from Samford, didn't lose a game. Apparently he is the only coach in Division I-A ever to go 11-0 in his rookie season.

If he isn't the national Coach of the Year, they should abolish the award.

If Auburn is the only undefeated, untied team when the last blitz is blitzed, it should be the national champion. Any voter in the AP poll who lets probation affect his choice shouldn't have a ballot.

Certainly Auburn is the SEC champion by any measuring stick— except the one that counts. Alabama vs. Florida for the title in Birmingham on Dec. 4 is a hollow game.

POWER SHIFT?

Another faddish question: Has the balance of power in the state shifted to Auburn? Oh, come on. Alabama lost a couple of games and tied one this year. Balances of power aren't sensitive to every little breeze. What we have are two superb programs, neither likely to murder the other on the field or in recruiting.

Where does this victory rank in the history of Auburn football?

All things considered, I'd rate the 30-20 win

When Bama was on offense, a roaring Auburn crowd forced quarterback Jay Barker to resort to hand signals early in the game.
Bernard Troncale photo

over Alabama in 1989 the biggest. Bama had sneered that it would never play at Auburn, but it not only did, it got whipped. The 23-22 victory over the Tide in 1982 broke a nine-Iron Bowl drought, and I'd put it second.

I believe this is No. 3, for it caps an undefeated season, it was against Auburn's top rival—which trumpeted its 1992 national title until the trumpets wore out—and it showed you can't keep a good man down by putting him on probation.

As they say, living well is the best revenge.

The deuce...was not loose; Auburn defenders saw to it.
Mark Almond photo

Auburn tailback Stephen Davis pulls away from Alabama end Dameian Jeffries.
Mark Almond photo

Bowden: 'It's everything I could ever imagine'

Neal Sims News staff writer

AUBURN—Terry Bowden finally saw his first Auburn-Alabama football game. And he won it.

"This is the biggest thing I've ever been a part of, this season and this game," said Bowden, who ended his first year as Auburn's head coach Saturday with a perfect record and a 22-14 victory over Alabama, then knelt at midfield with his predecessor Pat Dye in front of the cheering throng of Tigers' fans at Jordan-Hare Stadium.

"This is my 10th year as head football coach, and I've never been 11-0," said Bowden. "It's the

Auburn quarterback Stan White lofts a pass over Bama defenders; he was 11 for 26 on the day.
Mark Almond photo

greatest thrill in the world. I feel like an Auburn man. I guess I'm one now."

Bowden took a microphone to address the crowd, and with his arm around Dye, said to the fans, "We owe this game to one person, and that's coach Pat Dye."

Later, in his postgame interview, Bowden said of Dye, "Coming to Auburn, if he had not accepted me and publicly and privately said he was proud that I was here, I couldn't have made it. He turned it over to me. He gave his young men to me. Any time you see a man go through all the things he went through, for whatever reasons, your heart feels for a fellow coach."

The victory and this remarkable season will always be special to Auburn and to these players, said Bowden.

"These young men probably went to the lowest you could go as far as their heart because of all the things that pushed Auburn down," he said, refer-

ring to the long NCAA investigation and eventual sanctions against the Auburn football program. "For them to be driven down that low, then to be lifted to the heights of 11-0, their lives have changed."

Bowden said he didn't get caught up in the intensity of the rivalry until the weekend. "I was fine until Friday night," he said. "I was very relaxed. Then it hit me. I didn't sleep well. I was nervous all day. It's everything I could ever imagine.

"The game went exactly like I wanted it to go and hoped it would go but thought it wasn't going to go," added Bowden. "We played conservative. I felt like with their outstanding defense, we would make a mistake and get ourselves into trouble early. So I was going to be conservative."

Then the Tigers fell nine behind after two big scoring plays by Alabama and went to the locker room at halftime trailing 14-5.

"I asked the players to believe in themselves

and believe that somebody was going to make something happen to win.

"It's like it's been all year. I don't think we were the best athletes on the field. I was scared to death. They looked so strong. But we played as a team, and the team won. I guess it was just meant to be."

Patrick Nix, the backup quarterback, connected with wideout Frank Sanders for a touchdown pass on Nix' first play after starter Stan White was knocked out with a knee injury. Later, after a Scott Etheridge field goal, tailback James Bostic busted a 70-yard touchdown run.

"You give Bostic enough at-bats, and it's going to happen," said Bowden.

As for Nix, he said, "Patrick represents everything this team is about. I'm so proud of him, how he sat back and cheered Stan on, never getting his chance. Then he goes into the last game and throws the touchdown pass. It gives him a good po-

sition for the future and made a special day for him, too.

"This team has a special chemistry," added Bowden. "It's a game played with heart on top of the talent. It's a great team, and the emphasis is on team.

"I feel like if you put us on the field with anybody in the country, this team would find a way to keep it close and do something in the fourth quarter to win. I wouldn't begin to tell you how we would do it. I don't know."

What's next for the coach after a perfect start?

"We go out and recruit and we build a national champion," said Bowden. "The best way to build a program is to have total confidence that this is the direction we need to go and this is how we're going to get it done. I hope we didn't leave any doubt."

Auburn linebacker Jason Miska and others close in on Bama quarterback Jay Barker for a safety.
Mark Almond photo

White limps off, Nix comes on... touchdown

Kevin Scarbinsky, News columnist

AUBURN—They were down. Down on the scoreboard. Down on the field. Down in the third quarter, almost the last quarter of their last game in their own house. So close to the perfect ending to the perfect season, and the sun was going down on the Auburn Tigers.

Two temporary medics were helping quarterback Stan White limp to the sideline for good with a damaged knee ligament, a cruel end to his season of redemption. Police were about to issue a missing-persons report on the Auburn offense, whose streak of failing to score a touchdown against Alabama had reached 39 minutes on the clock, three years on the calendar.

The lead, Alabama winning 14-5, and the moment, Auburn facing fourth-and-15 at the Alabama 35-yard line, and the game seemed to belong to the Crimson Tide.

But what's a nine-point hole when you've

Alabama end Jeremy Nunley comes around Auburn tackle Anthony Redmond, but too late as Stan White passes the football just over the outstretched hands of Bama linebacker Andre Royal.
Joe Songer photo

*Auburn linebacker Jason Miska gets face to face with Alabama tail-
back Chris Anderson, as referee pushes them apart.*
Mark Almond photo

your head coach and your fearsome reputation and your respect from the rest of the league before the season even began? What's the heat of the moment when your entire program has walked across hot coals for two years?

Down? Auburn had been there. Auburn didn't like it. Auburn stood up, and just now backup quarterback Patrick Nix did the same. He stood up, raised up and floated a fourth-down rainbow toward the goal line, where Auburn receiver Frank Sanders and Alabama defender Tommy Johnson and the fate of the game awaited.

"I guess you call it a fairy tale," Auburn coach and mythmaker Terry Bowden said. "Isn't that what you call it?"

You might have called it an incomplete pass, a forgettable moment in yet another humdrum Alabama win over Auburn, if the Alabama defender had been Antonio Langham instead of Johnson. As Auburn receivers coach Tommy Bowden said, "They're both good players, but that one guy is going to be a millionaire."

Langham is that guy, and he was the guy who doubled as Sanders' shadow for most of the game. Sanders is Auburn's best receiver. Langham is the college game's best defensive back. Where Sanders went, Langham followed. Until the moment down became up and Auburn came alive, Sanders owned just three catches because Langham owned Sanders. Auburn expected Langham to follow Sanders again on fourth-and-15 at the Alabama 35, but Auburn didn't have much choice. The Tigers were too far away to kick a field goal into the wind but too close to punt, and Nix does not have the arm strength of White to throw across the field. So the Bowden brothers conjured what Tommy called "the safest throw," a lob pass straight down the field to the short side.

trailed explosive Florida by 13? What's a wounded quarterback and an ailing offense when you lost

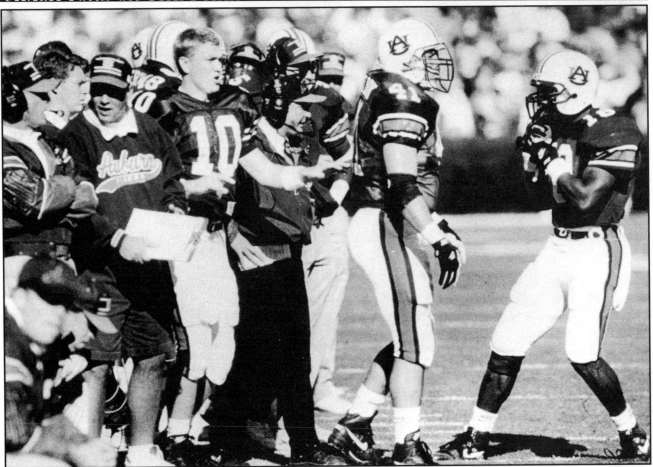

Coach Terry Bowden directs sideline traffic with Thomas Bailey (18) heading off the field and fullback Reid McMilion heading on the field.
Mark Almond photo

As Sanders ran to position, Langham started to follow but something stopped him halfway across the field, and he retreated to the wide side of the coverage. Langham usually plays the wide side where a defender does not have the sideline for help. Tommy Bowden's reaction in the press box when Langham turned away from Sanders' side: "Delight. I was happy."

No one should have been surprised. For an entire season, the small decisions that turn little moments into memories have all fallen Auburn's way.

And so Nix threw his lob pass and Sanders timed his jump and Auburn had its first touchdown against Alabama in three years and its first life against Alabama since early in the game. The lead would come later, followed by the perfect 22-14 ending to the perfect 11-0 season. But that one play when Nix came in cold and Langham turned the other way proved once and for all that this is an Auburn team blessed by hard work and talent but touched by something more.

Tommy Bowden, six times an assistant in this special game and six times a loser before Saturday, tried to give that something a name: "Magic. Fate. I'd say that had something to do with it. Fate. Luck. Whatever."

When their starting quarterback went down, it looked like bad luck, cruel fate. When their backup quarterback stepped up and threw a touchdown pass on his first pass while the best defensive back in the college game chose the other side of the field, it looked like something greater than hard work and talent. It looked like luck ... fate ... magic.

"I don't know how to explain it," said Terry Bowden, who has no need to explain. "Maybe it was just meant to be."

Tommy Bowden called play that turned the game

From staff reports

AUBURN—Patrick Nix called the play of the game "a prayer."

He was partly right. The play did come down to the field from up above.

Nix's 35-yard touchdown pass to Frank Sanders in the third quarter keyed the Tigers' 22-14 win over Alabama, the finishing touch on Auburn's unbeaten season.

It was the play of the game.

Nix came on with 6:22 left in the period after starter Stan White was carried off the field with a knee injury. Nix was surprised to be on the field. After all, it was fourth and 15. He figured the call would be a field goal attempt or a pooch punt into a stiff wind.

Auburn head coach Terry Bowden said he considered a punt. But in the Tiger coaches booth, high above the field, Tommy Bowden, the head coach's brother and Auburn's receivers coach, argued for a pass.

Terry Bowden agreed and called for the pass. The play is called 78 Z Stay Takeoff. Sanders lined up on the left sideline and went straight upfield.

"Frank told me, 'You get it up there and I'll catch it'," Nix said. "It was a playground pass."

It was also a successful pass. The 6-foot-2 Sanders outjumped 5-10 Alabama cornerback Tommy Johnson at the 4, caught the pass and dove into the end zone. "I just muscled him out of the way," Sanders said.

As the play began to develop, Tommy Bowden

Gallops like this by tailback James Bostic broke the heart and the back of the Crimson Tide.
Joe Songer photo

A frustrated Gene Stallings tries to rally his defense as the tide begins to turn in Auburn's favor during the third quarter.

Joe Songer photo

was worried it might not work. Bowden saw Alabama's All-America cornerback Antonio Langham starting to move over to cover Sanders.

"Langham was coming over, then turned around and went back to the other side of the field," Tommy Bowden said. He added that Langham "is going to be a millionaire (in the pros). I was so happy (he went back to the other side)."

The play turned the game back to Auburn's side. The Tigers still trailed 14-12, but now they had momentum.

White feels great after Nix's TD pass

Neal Sims, News staff writer

AUBURN—Mission accomplished.

Stan White, wounded in battle, had won the war. He was limping on crutches, but he wore the glow of the victor.

"I was going to stay out there with the fans as long as I could," said White after his final game at Auburn. "I don't care if I fall over.

"The pain in my knee can't spoil the joy I'm feeling," added Auburn's starting quarterback, who went down with a knee injury in the third quarter against Alabama Saturday.

Patrick Nix, for three years White's backup, came on and threw a 35-yard touchdown on the next play, a fourth-down score that launched the Tigers on their way to a 22-14 victory.

"The past is the past," said White, who after a sensational freshman season endured two years of the hardships faced by an Auburn team under NCAA scrutiny. He finished with an unbeaten 11-0 team. "I'm just going to enjoy this season and look back on my career at Auburn as being a success in my eyes.

"It's disappointing being hurt in my last game, but this is the best one I've been involved in at Auburn. I'll relish it for a while." White suffered either a torn or stretched ligament in his left knee. He will be evaluated by Dr. Larry Lemak at HealthSouth in Birmingham on Monday, but surgery is unlikely.

It was Lemak, administering to White on the sidelines, who told him Nix had thrown the TD toss.

"There's nothing better right now than to be a part of this," said Nix. "It's been tough for us. We fought through it, and now look where we are."

As for the pass, Nix said coach Terry Bowden told him just to throw it high for wideout Frank Sanders.

"I went and got my helmet. I didn't even loosen up. I looked Frank straight in the eye and said, "Just go catch it. I'm going to put it up there,' " said Nix. "I didn't have any doubt in the world that Frank could catch it. Tony Richardson told the line to protect me, and they did. I had the smallest role of the whole play.

"I was a little heartbroken because me and Stan have been through a lot together," Nix said of White's injury. "It was tough seeing him hurt. I've been under him for three years now. I look up to him. I really wanted him to finish this season off and beat Alabama himself. I still believe he would have beaten Alabama himself. But he got hurt, and I'm just glad I got to come in and beat Alabama for him."

Kicker Scott Etheridge (43) celebrates his first field goal of the game with holder Sean Carder
Mark Almond photo

It's time to party at Auburn

Ron Ingram, News staff writer

AUBURN—Don't expect the band to play "The Party's Over" for a long, long time in Auburn.

In fact, the celebration following Auburn's 22-14 victory over Alabama was as impressive as the team that went 11-0.

Moments after the final horn, Auburn coach Terry Bowden ran excitedly from sideline to sideline as the capacity Auburn crowd cheered in unison.

But that was just the beginning.

After the coaches and players spent some private time in the dressing room, the party rolled back out onto the Jordan-Hare Stadium carpet. And it was quite a party.

Enterprise senior Greg Thompson smoked a cigar. Joe Frazier and Wayne Gandy bounced and slid on the the banner that draped War Eagle over the 50-yard line. Lewis Battle went from hostess to hostess hugging necks as fans continued to cheer from their seats.

"I can tell you this is one celebration we aren't going to stop any time soon," said Thompson. Sophomore tight end Derrick Dorn tried to hide his cigar from his mother. But then he said what the heck.

"Coach Bowden passed them out to us," said Dorn. "I don't like cigars but I'm going to smoke this one."

Dorn said the 11-0 season still seemed like a dream.

"This was the finishing touch," he said.

The players continued to roam the stadium 45 minutes after the game had ended. And more than half the fans remained to continue cheering at the top of their lungs.

Freshman lineman Willie Anderson just smiled. "This is a great day to be from Auburn," he said as he finally headed for the dressing room a final time.

Auburn's sorrow . . .

Former Auburn strong safety Clarence Morton was on the mind of Auburn sideline radio announcer Quentin Riggins, a former Tiger linebacker himself, as the 22-14 victory over Alabama came to an end Saturday.

Riggins was remembering Morton, who died in a car crash Friday night near Dadeville en route to Auburn for the game.

"Clarence was a great guy here and one of my best friends," said Riggins. " I wish he could have been here to celebrate this win."

Morton, a 23-year-old from Maplesville, lettered at Auburn from 1989-92. He was an all-state running back at Maplesville

Auburn free safety Brian Robinson knocks a pass away from Alabama end Chad Key.
Steve Barnette photo

Coach Bowden gives instructions to quarterback Stan White as back-up QB Patrick Nix listens in.
Steve Barnette photo

High School in 1988.

The Auburn players had Morton on their minds, too. Running back James Bostic wore a wrist band with Morton's No. 13. Many of the players took a special moment to comfort current Tigers running back Harold Morrow, who is also from Maplesville and Morton's cousin.

"I couldn't believe it at first," said Wayne Gandy. "I played four years with him and he was a great friend."

—Ron Ingram

Auburn's joy

Sheryl Bowden, dressed in the requisite orange and blue and sporting a button that said, "Beat Bama," was wiping the tears from her eyes as her husband chatted with the press.

"We never dreamed that it would be like this," Terry Bowden's 30-year-old wife said after Auburn completed an 11-0 run by beating Alabama. "Of course, we hoped it would be."

In best coaching lingo, she said she just "took them one game at a time."

Mrs. Bowden said she was wrung out by this game. "I've got nothing left," she commented. "I'm ready to go home and go to bed right now."

She had never attended an Auburn-Alabama game before this one.

"I just hadn't been around the rivalry, but it finally started hitting me like it hits other people. We didn't sleep much last night, and I was sick at my stomach today. I went up to the suite, and it was 'just don't talk to me.' I almost broke the suite window during the game."

Of course she wouldn't have predicted an 11-0 season, but she did expect success. "There was never 'we can't do it' or "it's our first year and we're in a different division.' Never that."

After Auburn beat Florida, the notion of an 11-0 season did flare in her mind, though. "We both sat around after the Florida game and said, "If we can beat Florida we can beat anybody.' "

The Bowdens are still living at Sewell Hall, the athletic dormitory.

Auburn assistants help an injured White from the field after he sustained a knee injury in the second half.
Steve Barnette photo

"My family and I have given up a lot of time," she said, "but it's been worth it. It's been a very special year."

Endorsement by Pat Dye, Bowden's predecessor, smoothed the way for her husband, she said. "Coach Dye accepted us. He offered any help he could. There was no animosity. He eats lunch with us once a week. He came up to me in the suite and gave me a big hug. He's a great guy."

Her husband, she said, "had been handling this game like 'any other game,' but last night he was reading the paper and wasn't reading it, just seeing black lines. The excitement level was so high.

"I don't know how people stood it when there was an off-week before this game."

Someone asked her age, and she replied: "Thirty going on 80."

—Clyde Bolton

Outside listening in

Probably nowhere have so many fans listened to a football game outside a stadium.

Thousands of Alabama and Auburn fans showed up here Saturday without tickets in hopes of finding a bargain, but bargains were virtually nonexistent at kickoff time. "I was going to listen to it on the radio anyway, so I just thought I'd come on up and see what the ticket prices were," said Louis Cole of Enterprise, who was among the thousands outside the stadium looking for tickets near kickoff time. "They were $500 a pair a few hours ago and they've dropped to $300 now, but I'm not going to pay that. I've got the car keys and a radio in the car."

Four tickets together on the 30-yard line were bringing $1,000 two hours before kickoff, said Birmingham's Lyle Funderburk, who scalps tickets to a variety of sporting events.

—Mike Bolton

A night of fun

From the crowd around Jordan Hare Stadium on Friday night, you might have figured everyone had arrived a day early for the Auburn-Alabama game.

It was a gathering like you'd see at New Orleans' French Quarter—thousands of revelers, cars and recreational vehicles end to end for blocks, and a night of fun.

The stadium lights stayed on well into the evening, and one bank was left on all night.

Virtually all but the reserved parking spots near the stadium were taken the night before the game. Fans sang, danced, cooked out and partied.

—*Neal Sims*

Seeing double or nothing

Closed circuit TV adds new episode to football saga

Mike Bolton and Doug Segrest
News staff writers

This often-bizarre football rivalry has seen everything from blocked punts to a state law forcing the two teams to play, but this year's Alabama-Auburn game took another strange twist.

The matchup will mark the first time in history

With White out of the game, Nix suddenly found himself on center stage where he receives quick instructions by headset from press box coaches.
Steve Barnette photo

that a college football game has sold out in two stadiums.

In Tuscaloosa, everything was in place Friday for the world's largest gathering of couch potatoes. A 20-by-28-foot television screen is anchored in the upper southwest corner of Bryant-Denny Stadium and a field-level, 14-foot-by-18-foot auxiliary screen sat in the end zone for 45,000 fans who would view the closed-circuit broadcast.

In Auburn, a sign proclaiming "The Second Coming—Welcome Back To Your Worst Nightmare" was one of hundreds that greeted severely outnumbered Alabama fans on the eve of what many believe is college football's fiercest rivalry.

It was Alabama's second visit to Jordan-Hare, capacity 85,214. The first was in 1989 when Auburn won 30-20.

Former Alabama residents Tommy and Peggy Sanford, of Panama City, Fla., couldn't wait until the weekend to get their game faces on. They rolled their Auburn memorabilia-clad motor home into the stadium parking lot on Monday.

"We were the first motor home here," Mrs. Sanford said.

Alabama fan Ken Kendrick of Atlanta found his motor home surrounded by a sea of orange and blue. Although greatly outnumbered, he staked his claim in the middle of a parking lot and proudly displayed his colors, including an elephant raising its trunk in triumph.

"I'm just trying to stay above it all," said Kendrick, whose mother and brother went to Auburn. "Somebody who was an Alabama fan walked by here last night, but they have been few and far between."

Renting, transporting and erecting the screens at Bryant-Denny stadium—the Jumbotron came from Gainesville, Fla., while the auxiliary screen was shipped from Belgium —will run "around $150,000," said Kirk Wood, executive director of Collegiate Sports Partners, Ltd.

Wood's Birmingham-based company, which owns rights to Alabama athletic broadcasts, leased the equipment for the broadcast and hired the broadcasting team.

The picture was darker than that of a normal television set and the clarity wasn't quite as good. But even fans sitting on the top row in the opposite end zone were able to see clearly.

Although some might have thought there was nothing left to do in the Auburn Athletic Department ticket office except count money—the game had been sold out since Auburn's second game in September—the phones were ringing off the hook all week.

"We've had people say they just were in the area visiting from California and wanted to know where to get tickets, and a lot wanting to know if we know of any individuals wanting to sell tickets," said assistant ticket manager Tim Garner.

Amazingly, one of those avoiding the pre-game commotion

Auburn receiver Frank Sanders and Alabama's Antonio Langham fight over the ball in the endzone.
Joe Songer photo

Auburn's Tony Richardson and Alabama's Antonio Langham come face-to-face.
Bernard Troncale photo

Friday was Bowden. Looking like a college student dressed in a pair of sweats with an Auburn logo, he jogged across campus virtually unnoticed by fans.

Tide gambled and lost with game on the line

Doug Segrest, News staff writer

AUBURN—Twice, Alabama gambled. Twice it was burned:

The first came on fourth-and-1 from its own 29-yard line with nine minutes left in the game.

Fullback Tarrant Lynch took the hand off and tried to dive over the top, but Auburn's defensive penetration cut him down for no gain.

The second came on an Auburn 1st and 10 from the AU 30 with 2:33 left. Trying to stifle the Tiger ground game and get the ball back, Alabama went to a goal-line defense, one James Bostic ripped through for a 70-yard touchdown.

Two plays didn't decide the game, but they told much of the story in Auburn's 22-14 victory over its arch-rival, one that should impress pollsters.

The fourth-and-1 call was made by Stallings, who figured his defense would keep Alabama in contention.

"I went for it," he said. "If I had it to do over again, I'd do it again. We had six inches to go and we didn't get it."

The decision didn't hurt Alabama, at least in terms of points. Auburn could not score.

But the Tigers did erase five critical minutes off

Auburn defensive tackles Randy Hart (98) and Damon Primus (77) celebrate with the crowd as Wayne Gandy waves a huge Auburn flag.
Steve Barnette photo

the clock between Lynch's dive for the first down and Alabama's next offensive possession.

The second gamble, on Auburn's next-to-last possession, was more basic. Alabama stacked the line of scrimmage, daring Auburn and backup quarterback Patrick Nix to throw the ball.

Auburn didn't, leaving the Tide wishing it had.

"We gambled on that goal-line defense," Gaston said. "But the weakness was in the middle, and they exploited it."

"We were just in the wrong defense at the wrong time," added defensive tackle Shannon Brown.

Alabama could spark little consistent offense. While it churned out 269 yards, it lost 117 in penalties.

Alabama's offense struggled in the second half, producing only 76 yards. The Tide's top offensive

weapon, David Palmer, was limited to four catches and an incompletion he threw on a flanker-around pass due to a collarbone injury. Starting quarterback Jay Barker completed 9 of 23 passes, throwing two interceptions, before leaving the game in the final minutes with what is likely a season-ending knee injury.

Tailback Sherman Williams, who rushed for five consecutive 100-yard games to open the year, saw limited action, gaining 12 yards on five carries. What spark there was for Alabama was provided by senior tailback Chris Anderson, who ran for 68 yards and caught one pass for 26 more.

"This was my best game, probably in a long time," he said. "I was healthy for a change, and I came in with my mind made up to take what they'd give me."

Meanwhile, the Tide defense gave up 351

Patrick Nix, who replaced Stan White and passed for a touchdown on his first play, holds tight to a game ball.
Bernard Troncale photo

FAIRHOPE PUBLIC LIBRARY

yards, 226 in the second half.

"We were on the field for a very long time," said defensive back Sam Shade. "But we're in good shape. We have no excuses." While many of the Tide players weren't ready to admit Auburn was the better team—"I feel we're better," said receiver Toderick Malone— Shade's perspective was a little more gracious.

"I congratulate Auburn. They've had a great season. I think we have, too, but not as good as we would've liked."

Tide fans watch Tiger Walk

Clyde Bolton, News staff writer

AUBURN—Alabama fans mingled with Auburn fans to watch the traditional Tiger Walk before the game Saturday. Thousands of fans stood 10 and 15 deep and perched on hills, motorhomes and the baseball field bleachers to watch Auburn's players walk several hundred yards from the athletic dormitory to the stadium.

Police reported no injuries and no incidents during the Tiger Walk. Auburn officials had expressed concern about the press of the throng after fans were hurt at a game at Wisconsin this season.

"It's very impressive," Charles McCaleb, an Alabama fan from Centreville, said of the Tiger Walk.

Alabama should move its games with Auburn from Birmingham to Tuscaloosa when the contract with Birmingham expires, he added.

Darrell Hobson, another Tide supporter from Centreville who accompanied McCaleb, said he thought the Tiger Walk was a good tradition. "I'm an Alabama fan," Hobson said, "but Terry Bowden has done a tremendous job."

Ruth Parker, an Auburn resident who was one day short of her 73rd birthday, observed the Tiger Walk. "I've been coming to Auburn games for 47 years," she said. "I go to the Tiger Walk because I love Auburn."

Mrs. Parker and her daughter, Marilyn Swaim, kept straight faces as they told inquirers that they were cooking elephant meat at their motorhome,

supposedly flown in from a gourmet shop in Tampa.

Five cookers were smoking under a funeral home awning at their motor home. Among a horde of Auburn fans, Alabama fan Morris Pate prepared Brunswick stew that included five chickens, two turkeys and six Boston butts. "We've been here since Wednesday," said Michael Klein. And where does he live? "In Auburn."

Bowden making pitch for No. 1

By Neal Sims
News staff writer

AUBURN— Destiny keeps turning Auburn's way, so why, figures coach Terry Bowden, won't it turn one more time.

This charmed football team has wrapped up it perfect season, finished now after a 22-14 victory over Alabama Saturday, and Auburn (11-0 overall, 8-0 in the Southeastern Conference) stands No. 3 in the nation.

So what's left? The national championship.

Bowden has begun his pitch.

He made it worldwide Sunday morning, telling CNN, "If we're the only undefeated team after the bowl games, I think they should rate us No. 1."

Auburn has no chance in the coaches' poll, which refuses to vote for a team on NCAA probation, but in the Associated Press poll of writers and sportscasters, the title remains a possibility.

"I'd love a split national championship," said Bowden, thinking of a family plan where father Bobby's Florida State team wins one and Auburn takes the other.

Before this past weekend, he acknowledged it was a long shot. "But I couldn't imagine Ohio State, Miami and Notre Dame losing," he said. "I said before you'd have to draw a pretty crooked line with your pencil for us to get there. Well, it's getting pretty crooked out there.

"I don't think you can take the championship without going to a bowl. But you can get it because the others went and lost."

This whole trip through the 1993 season has

Alabama and Auburn players embraced when the hard fought battle was ended, this time with the men in orange and blue accepting the congratulations.

been that way for Auburn.

"Now that it's over," said Bowden Sunday, in between his CNN telecast and a Sunday church service, "you can say you couldn't have imagined this. I would not have even wasted my time thinking about it.

"The Amazins' have been here," he said, referring to the 1972 Auburn team. "Maybe this team is The Unbelievables.

"Nobody should play us. There's something attached to this team. I don't know what it is. You don't want to play this team this year.

"The wind's going to knock your ball backward and we're going to catch it. The ground's going to cave in, you're going to fall in and we're going to score. The second-team quarterback comes off the bench without warming up and throws a touchdown pass on fourth-and-15. It's a charmed team.

"That's exactly why don't you think they could be No. 1. Pollsters, just hang on."

The ground hasn't caved in under an opponent yet, but that storybook scenario with the backup quarterback did unfold Saturday against Alabama. It's part of the Auburn lore of 1993.

"I don't want to take away from these players," said Bowden. "They play hard, and they have a lot of heart. This is a real type of Horatio Alger team. They worked their way up, and good fortune has come to them. It's like an angel is sitting on their shoulder, watching over them."

Ask Bowden how he did it, and he replied, "I'm young enough, excited enough and enthusiastic enough, thrilled enough to have the job, to have just brought back a little of that spark," he said. "I'm smart enough to hire coaches that can coach a little bit better than I can. And I'm pretty good at play-calling.

"We had a sound system. We played hard defensive football. We were as good as we could possibly be. On offense, we could block and we could execute.

"I've put an offense in that I've been running for 10 years. I know it from top to bottom. Every defense that you can stop it with, I've come up against at some time before." Against Alabama, though, Bowden said coaching wasn't what won it.

"I couldn't beat Brother Oliver," he said, referring to Alabama defensive chief Bill Oliver. "I saw what he was going to do to stop it. I knew what to do to counter it. But they were too good. He had me beat. What happened was the players came out and beat it.

"Brother Oliver is one of the best coaches in the country. He just totally had us. Wayne Hall (Auburn's defensive head coach) is out there on the other side of the ball. Both defensive coaches won. Every coach kind of neutralized each other, and the players had to go out and win the game.

"Coaches couldn't do it. It wasn't trick plays or fancy calls."

Bowden put the victory over Alabama in perspective.

"You're not going to beat them all the time," he said. "If I'm as good as the greatest coaches that ever coached here, I'll be lucky to get them half the time. That's going to be our job. That's the way it is with all great rivalries.

"That win was not all that important to the future of the program," he added. "Recruits come for a lot of reasons.

"We have done the most we can do to prepare us for the future. We could have gone 7-4, but 7-4 might not have convinced a recruit in South Florida, 7-4 might not have recruited the No. 1 player in Texas.

"Alabama and Auburn will always fight for the best ones in Alabama. We didn't take a step up on Alabama Saturday there. It's all even in this state, always will be in recruiting."

11-0 Auburn raises eyes far and wide

Kevin Scarbinsky
News columnist

First came a score. Michigan 14, Ohio State 0. And then came a cheer.

Then came another score. Boston College 10, Notre Dame 0. And then came another cheer.

There would be more scores from Ann Arbor, Mich., and South Bend, Ind., and there would be more cheers in Auburn, Ala.

Auburn was playing Alabama, and if ever an entire state puts on blinders for one game on one fall afternoon, this is the state and this is the game. But on this fall afternoon, even as they rejoiced over what they saw with their own eyes in their own house, the Auburn fans took off their blinders and reveled in what they heard with their own ears.

The in-house reaction to Auburn 22, Alabama 14 and Victories 11, Defeats 0 was a celebration. History is not make and justice is not done and Alabama is not beaten every day.

The in-house reaction to the favorable scores from distant shores was a revelation. Even as it was looking down on Alabama for the first time in four years, Auburn could see beyond Alabama. There was a bigger bear in the woods, and Auburn was raising its sights to the national championship.

IN THE SPOTLIGHT

It doesn't matter whether Auburn actually wins the national championship because no poll can measure the significance of what this team has accomplished. It does matter that the polls and Auburn matter to one another again because one of Terry Bowden's most important accomplishments has been to open Auburn's eyes to the nation and to open the nation's eyes to Auburn.

First the spotlight came because of his name.

It was gilt by association, an accident of birth in which his father would become one of the game's best coaches at Florida State. Bowden was a national name before Terry won a single Division I-A game. Auburn was a regional place that a lot of people who never ate grits thought was in the state of Georgia.

But as the season and the legend grew, the fame focused more on Bowden's environment and less on his heredity. ESPN and CNN and company came calling because one of the best football teams in the land lives in Auburn.

In the past, when the outside world thought of college football in this state, most of the time it thought of Alabama. In the future, Auburn will find itself alongside Alabama on the national stage, most of the news will be good and the state's image will be doubly blessed.

NO. 1 NOT IMPOSSIBLE

For Auburn, the No. 3 football team in the land according to the AP poll, the future starts now. In the space of 24 hours this weekend, Oklahoma could beat No. 2 Nebraska and Florida could beat No. 1 Florida State and Auburn could be alone at the top.

Is that impossible, incredible, insane? No more so that Notre Dame beating Florida State one week and losing to Boston College the next. Or unbeaten Ohio State losing by four touchdowns to mediocre Michigan. Or three of the five teams who were ranked ahead of Auburn last week -- Notre Dame, Ohio State and Miami -- all losing Saturday.

Maybe Auburn is fortunate that its dream season ended on the field with a win over the opponent that mattered most to the most Auburn people. Two games left to play would have meant two more chances to see reality intrude on the dream.

More likely, it is the teams Auburn would have played in the SEC Championship Game and the Sugar Bowl who are fortunate. Is Auburn the best team in the country? If the Tigers can't prove they are, no one else can prove they're not.

Alabama	0	14	0	0 — 14
Auburn	3	2	7	10 — 22

First Quarter
Aub—Etheridge 23 FG

Second Quarter
Ala—Lee 63 run (Proctor kick)

Aub—Barker sacked by Miska for safety

Ala—Anderson 19 run (Proctor kick)

Third Quarter
Aub—Sanders 35 pass from Nix (Etheridge kick)

Fourth Quarter
Aub—Etheridge 26 FG

Aub—Bostic 70 run (Etheridge kick)

Attendance— 85,214

	Ala	Aub
First downs	10	22
Rushes-yards	26-113	51-218
Passing	156	133
Return Yards	23	69
Comp-Att-Int	10-29-2	14-29-1
Punts	7-47	7-41
Fumbles-Lost	0-0	0-0
Penalties-Yards	12-117	4-37
Time of Possession	21:44	38:16

INDIVIDUALS
ALABAMA

Rushing

Player	Att.	Yds.	TD	Long
Barker	4	-25	0	-1
Anderson	10	68	1	19
Lynch	4	5	0	3
Lee	1	63	1	63
Williams	5	12	0	4
Burgdorf	2	-12	0	-5

Passing

Player	A-C-I	Yds	TD	Long
Barker	23-9-2	130	0	34
Palmer	1-0-0	0	0	0
Burgdorf	5-1-0	26	0	26

Receiving

Player	No.	Yds	TD	Long
Palmer	4	60	0	28
Johnson	1	5	0	5
Lynch	1	11	0	11
Lee	2	39	0	34
Key	1	15	0	15
Anderson	1	26	0	26

Punting

Player	No.	Yds	Avg	Long
Diehl	7	328	46.8	68

Returns

Player	Punts	Kickoff	Int.
Palmer	3-23	4-74	
Gaston			1-0

AUBURN

Rushing

Player	Att.	Yds.	TD	Long
White	10	23	0	11
Bostic	19	147	1	70
Richardson	10	25	0	5
Davis	6	13	0	15
McMillon	3	12	0	8
Nix	2	-2	0	1
Carder	1	0	0	0

Passing

Player	A-C-I	Yds	TD	Long
White	26-11-1	85	0	16
Nix	3-3-0	50	1	35

Receiving

Player	No.	Yds	TD	Long
McMillon	1	6	0	6
Bailey	2	25	0	15
Sanders	5	75	1	35
Richardson	3	28	0	15
Bostic	1	-5	0	-5
Davis	1	0	0	0
Dorn	1	4	0	4

Punting

Player	No.	Yds	Avg	Long
Daniel	7	289	41.3	49

Returns

Player	Punts	Kickoff	Int.
Bailey	4-52	1-22	
Robinson			1-17
McGee			1-0

DEFENSE
ALABAMA

Tackles, assists — T.P.Johnson 4-1; Hall 7-3; W.Brown 2-1; Donnelly 0-1; Gaston 6-4; Shade 4-2; Royal 6-0; Turner 0-1; Conn 1-0; Langham 4-0; Rogers 4-6; Morris 4-1; Nunley 7-3; S.Brown 2-0; Powell 1-0; Walters 3-1; Jeffries 0-1; Gregory 2-2; Blackburn 1-0; Davis 0-1; Diehl 1-0; Floyd 1-0; Torrence 0-1; E.Brown 1-0.
Sacks — Royal, Nunley. Fumbles recovered — None. Passes intercepted — Gaston. Passes broken up — Gaston, Langham.

AUBURN

Tackles, assists — Shelling 5-1; Jackson 1-2; Robinson 3-1; Pina 4-4; Solomon 5-5; Miska 6-6; Pelton 3-1; Harris 3-6; Thornton 1-0; Primus 0-2; Whitehead 1-1; Walker 1-2; Hart 1-0; Crook 2-0; Etheridge 2-0; Frazier 1-0; Malcom 1-0; Brinsfield 1-0.
Sacks — Pelton, Harris 2, Whitehead, Miska. Fumbles recovered — None. Passes intercepted — B.Robinson, McGee. Passes broken up — B.Robinson, Shelling, Jackson.

AUBURN SEASON
Results (11-0)

Sept. 2	Ole Miss,	Won 16-12
Sept. 11	Samford,	Won 35-7
Sept. 18	at LSU,	Won 34-10
Sept. 25	Southern Miss,	Won 35-24
Oct. 2	at Vandy,	Won 14-10
Oct. 9	Miss. State,	Won 31-17
Oct. 16	Florida,	Won 38-35
Oct. 30	at Arkansas,	Won 38-21
Nov. 6	New Mexico St.,	Won 55-14
Nov. 13	at Georgia,	Won 42-28
Nov. 20	Alabama,	Won 22-14

Auburn vs. Alabama Jordan-Hare Stadium

Play-by-play

FIRST QUARTER

November 20, 1993—Auburn wins the toss and defers. Auburn defends the north goal.

Bryan Karkoska kicks off to David Palmer at the Alabama 5-yard line. Palmer returns 18 yards then is stopped by Auburn's Kelsey Crook at the Alabama 23.

1st and 10 - UA23 - Chris Anderson runs at right end for 6 yards. Tackled by Jason Miska and Derrick Robinson

2nd and 4 - UA29 - David Palmer's pass to Chad Key is incomplete. Broken up by Derrick Robinson.

3rd and 4 - UA29 - Tarrant Lynch runs at right end for 2 yards. Tackled by Scott Etheridge and Terry Solomon.

4th and 2 - UA31 - Bryne Diehl punts 41 yards to Thomas Bailey at the Auburn 28. Bailey returns 4 yards. No tackle.

POSSESSION TO AUBURN (with 13:29 remaining)

1st and 10 - AU32 - James Bostic runs at center for 2 yards. Tackled by Sam Shade.

2nd and 8 - AU34 - Toss to James Bostic at right end. Offsetting penalties. Replay down.

2nd and 8 - AU34 - Tony Richardson runs at left end for 5 yards. Tackled by Willie Gaston and Eric Turner.

3rd and 3 - AU39 - Stan White sacked by Andre Royal for 9-yard loss.

4th and 12-AU30 - Terry Daniel punts 45 yards to David Palmer at the Alabama 25. Five-yard return.

POSSESSION TO ALABAMA (with 10:59 remaining)

1st and 10 - UA30 - Chris Anderson runs at center for 1 yard. Tackled by Terry Solomon and Anthony Harris.

2nd and 9 - UA31 - Jay Barker completes 3-yard pass to David Palmer. Chris Shelling makes stop.

3rd and 6 - UA34 - Penalty against Alabama (illegal procedure - 5 yards)

3rd and 11-UA29 - Jay Barker incomplete to David Palmer.

4th and 11-UA29 - Bryne Diehl punts 34 yards, out of bounds at the Auburn 38.

POSSESSION TO AUBURN (with 9:07 remaining)

1st and 10 - AU38 - Stan White runs around right end for 8 yards. Tackled by Willie Gaston.

2nd and 2 - AU46 - Tony Richardson runs at left guard for 2 yards. Tackled by Willie Gaston and Mario Morris.

1st and 10 - AU48 - Stan White runs out of pocket for 2 yards. Andre Royal makes tackle.

2nd and 8 - AU50 - James Bostic stopped at line of scrimmage for 1-yard loss. Tackled by James Gregory and Elverett Brown.

3rd and 9 - AU49 - Stan White completes 15-yard pass to Tony Richardson. Lemanski Hall makes tackle.

1st and 10 - UA36 - Stan White completes to James Bostic, but loses 5 yards. Tackled by Andre Royal.

2nd and 15-UA41 - Stan White completes 6-yard pass to Reid McMilion. Andre Royal and Michael Rogers make stop.

3rd and 9 - UA35 - Stan White pass incomplete to Thomas Bailey.

4th and 9 - UA35 - Scott Etheridge's 52-yard field goal attempt is no good. But Alabama penalty (illegal substitution - 15 yards) retains Auburn possession.

1st and 10 -UA20 - James Bostic runs at right guard for 2 yards. Stopped by Sam Shade and Michael Rogers.

2nd and 8 - UA18 - Stan White keeps, runs up middle for 7 yards. Tackle by Michael Rogers.

3rd and 1 - UA11 - Stan White keeps, runs up middle for 4 yards. James Gregory tackles.

1st and G - UA7 - Tony Richardson runs at left guard for 1 yard. Sam Shade and Mario Morris make tackle.

2nd and G- UA6 - Stan White pass incomplete

to Tony Richardson.

3rd and G - UA6 - Stan White pass incomplete to Frank Sanders.

4th and G - UA6 - Scott Etheridge kicks 23-yard field goal (with 1:48 remaining)

SCORE - Auburn 3, Alabama 0

DRIVE - Three plays, 56 yards, 7:19

Bryan Karkoska kicks off to David Palmer at the Alabama 6. Palmer returns 17 yards.

POSSESSION TO ALABAMA (with 1:43 remaining)

1st and 10 - UA23 - Chris Anderson runs at right end for 12 yards. Mike Pina makes stop.

1st and 10 - UA35 - Chris Anderson runs at left guard, but penalty on Alabama (illegal procedure - 5 yards)

1st and 15 - UA30 - Jay Barker completes 28-yard pass to David Palmer. Jason Miska makes tackle.

1st and 10 - AU42 - Eric Turner runs at center, but penalty on Alabama (illegal procedure - 5 yards)

1st and 15 - AU47 - Jay Barker completes 6-yard pass to David Palmer. Terry Solomon and Mike Pelton make stop.

2nd and 9 - AU41 - Time runs out. End of first quarter

SCORE: Auburn 3, Alabama 0

SECOND QUARTER

2nd and 9 - AU41 - Jay Barker completes 5-yard pass to Tony Johnson. Terry Solomon and Marc Johnson make tackle.

3rd and 4 - AU36 - Jay Barker incomplete to Kevin Lee.

4th and 4 - AU36 - Bryne Diehl punts 36 yards to the endzone. Touchback.

POSSESSION TO AUBURN (with 13:57 remaining)

1st and 10 - AU20 - Stephen Davis runs at left guard for 15 yards. Tackled by Tommy Johnson.

1st and 10 - AU35 - Stephen Davis runs up middle. No gain. Lemanski Hall makes stop.

2nd and 10-AU35 - Stan White completes 10-yard pass to Thomas Bailey. Tackle by T o m m y

Johnson.

1st and 10 - AU45 - Stan White incomplete to Sean Carder.

2nd and 10-AU45 - Stan White shuffles to Stephen Davis. No gain. Tackle by Lemanski Hall.

3rd and 10-AU45 - Stephen Davis tackled by Andre Royal for 6-yard loss.

4th and 16-AU39 - Terry Daniel punts 39 yards to David Palmer at Alabama 21. Palmer returns 8 yards. Tackled by Anthony Harris and Roymon Malcolm.

POSSESSION TO ALABAMA (with 10:49 remaining)

1st and 10 - UA29 - Toss to Chris Anderson at left tackle, 8-yard gain. Stopped by Mike Pelton and Chris Shelling.

2nd and 2 - UA37 - Reverse to Kevin Lee, around right end for 63-yard touchdown (with 10:00 remaining). Michael Proctor kicks extra point.

SCORE: Alabama 7, Auburn 3

DRIVE: Two plays, 71 yards, 0:49

William Watts kicks off to Thomas Bailey in endzone. Touchback.

POSSESSION TO AUBURN (with 10:00 remaining)

1st and 10 - AU20 - James Bostic runs up middle for 4 yards. Lemanski Hall and Sam Shade make tackle.

2nd and 6 - AU24 - Stan White completes 15-yard pass to Thomas Bailey. No tackle.

1st and 10 - AU39 - Tony Richardson runs 1 yard at center. Andre Royal tackles.

2nd and 9 - AU40 - Stan White completes to Tony Richardson for 4 yards. Antonio Langham makes stop.

3rd and 5 - AU44 - Tony Richardson runs 1 yard at center. Sam Shade and Jeremy Nunley make tackle.

4th and 4 - AU45 - Terry Daniel punts 49 yards to the Alabama 6. Ball is downed.

POSSESSION TO ALABAMA (with 7:05 remaining)

1st and 10 - UA6 - Jay Barker pass incomplete to Kevin Lee.

2nd and 10-UA6 - Jason Miska sacks Jay Barker in endzone for 6-yard loss and safety (with 6:52 remaining).

SCORE: Alabama 7, Auburn 5

Bryne Diehl punts to Dell McGee. Out of bounds at Auburn 41.

POSSESSION TO AUBURN (with 6:52 remaining)

1st and 10 - AU41 - Stan White tackled by Darrell Blackburn. No gain.

2nd and 10-AU41 - Stan White completes 4-yard pass to Frank Sanders. Mario Morris makes tackle.

3rd and 6 - AU45 - Stan White keeps, runs 7 yards up middle. Will Brown tackles.

1st and 10- UA48 - Stan White deep pass incomplete.

2nd and 10-UA48 - James Bostic runs at left guard, loses 1 yard. Penalty on Auburn (holding is declined).

3rd and 11-UA49 - Stan White pass incomplete to Tony Richardson. (Holding penalty declined).

4th and 11-UA49 - Terry Daniel punts 34 yards to David Palmer at Alabama 15. Palmer returns 10 yards. Penalty on Alabama (illegal block in back).

POSSESSION TO ALABAMA (with 4:05 remaining)

1st and 10 - UA15 - Penalty on Alabama (illegal motion - 5 yards)

1st and 15 - UA10 - Chris Anderson runs 1 yard at center. Mike Pelton, Jason Miska and Anthony Harris make tackle.

2nd and 14-UA11 - Jay Barker completes 11-yard pass to Tarrant Lynch. Stopped by Calvin Jackson.

3rd and 3 - UA22 - Jay Barker pass incomplete. Mike Pelton pressures.

4th and 3 - UA22 - Bryne Diehl punts 68 yards to Thomas Bailey at the Auburn 10. Bailey returns 10 yards. Will Brown makes stop.

POSSESSION TO AUBURN (with 2:41 remaining)

1st and 10 - AU20 - Stephen Davis runs 1 yard at center. Tackled by Lemanski Hall and Michael Rogers.

2nd and 9 - AU21 - Stephen Davis runs 1 yard at right end.

3rd and 8 - AU22 - Stephen Davis runs 2 yards at left end. Michael Rogers makes stop.

4th and 6 - AU24 - Terry Daniel punts 29 yards. Out of bounds at Alabama 47.

POSSESSION TO ALABAMA (with 1:30 remaining)

1st and 10 - UA47 - Jay Barker completes 34-yard pass to Kevin Lee. Calvin Jackson tackles.

1st and 10 - AU19 - Chris Anderson runs 19 yards around left end for touchdown (with 1:08 remaining). Michael Proctor kicks extra point.

SCORE: Alabama 14, Auburn 5.
DRIVE: Two plays, 53 yards, 0:22

William Watts kicks off to Thomas Bailey at the goal line. Bailey returns 22 yards, stopped by Mickey Conn and Fernando Davis.

POSSESSION TO AUBURN (with 1:01 remaining)

1st and 10 - AU22 - James Bostic runs 14 yards around left end. Shannon Brown stops.

1st and 10 - AU36 - Stan White completes 12-yard pass to Frank Sanders. Penalty on Alabama (personal foul - 15 yards).

1st and 10 - UA35 - Stan White pass incomplete.

2nd and 10-UA35 - Stan White pass to Thomas Bailey incomplete.

3rd and 10-UA35 - Penalty on Auburn (illegal motion - 5 yards).

3rd and 15-UA40 - Stan White keeps, loses 1 yard.

4th and 16-UA41 - Stan White pass incomplete to Frank Sanders. Penalty on Alabama (pass interference - 12 yards).

1st and 10 - UA29 - Stan White pass incomplete. End of half.

HALFTIME SCORE: Alabama 14, Auburn 5.

THIRD QUARTER

Auburn will receive. Alabama will kick off and defend the north goal. William Watts kicks off through the endzone. Touchback.

POSSESSION TO AUBURN

1st and 10 - AU20 - Stan White pass incomplete to Thomas Bailey.

2nd and 10 - AU20 - Stan White pass incomplete to Thomas Bailey.

3rd and 10 - AU20 - Stan White pass incomplete to Thomas Bailey. Jeremy Nunley pressures.

4th and 10 - AU20 - Terry Daniel punts 44 yards to Alabama 36. Ball is downed.

POSSESSION TO ALABAMA (with 14:35 remaining)

1st and 10 - UA36 - Chris Anderson runs 9 yards up middle. Tackled by Mike Pina.

2nd and 1 - UA46 - Tarrant Lynch runs 2 yards at center. Alonzo Etheridge tackles.

1st and 10 - AU48 - Chris Anderson runs 7 yards at right guard. Stopped by Mike Pina.

2nd and 3 - AU45 - Chris Anderson runs up middle. Penalty on Alabama (holding - 10 yards).

2nd and 13 - UA45 - Jay Barker dropped for 9-yard loss by Mike Pelton, Willie Whitehead and Anthony Harris.

3rd and 22 - UA36 - Jay Barker is sacked by Anthony Harris for 7-yard loss.

4th and 29 - UA29 - Bryne Diehl punts 45 yards to Thomas Bailey at Auburn 26. Bailey returns 30 yards. Tackled by Diehl.

POSSESSION TO AUBURN (with 11:38 remaining)

1st and 10 - UA44 - Stan White pass incomplete to Thomas Bailey.

2nd and 10- UA44 - Stan White pass intercepted by Willie Gaston (intended for Sean Carder) at the Alabama 27. Penalty on Alabama (unsportsmanlike conduct - 15 yards).

POSSESSION TO ALABAMA (with 11:17 remaining)

1st and 10 - UA13 - Sherman Williams runs for 3 yards at left guard. Tackled by Terry Solomon and Jason Miska.

2nd and 7 - UA16 - Toss to Sherman Williams. No gain. Stopped by Chris Shelling.

3rd and 7 - UA16 - Jay Barker pass to Kevin Lee incomplete.

4th and 7 - UA16 - Bryne Diehl punts 65 yards

to Thomas Bailey at Auburn 19. Bailey returns 8 yards. Stopped by Lamont Floyd.

POSSESSION TO AUBURN (with 9:42 remaining)

1st and 10 - AU27 - Stan White pass incomplete to Frank Sanders. Antonio Langham deflects pass attempt.

2nd and 10 - AU27 - James Bostic runs 4 yards at right guard. James Gregory tackles.

3rd and 6 - AU31 - Stan White keeps for 11 yards. Tackled by Lemanski Hall.

1st and 10 - AU42 - Stan White passes for 4 yards to Derrick Dorn. No tackle.

2nd and 6 - AU46 - Reid McMilion runs 8 yards up middle. Jeremy Nunley tackles.

1st and 10 - UA46 - Stan White completes to Frank Sanders for 16 yards. Tackled by Antonio Langham.

1st and 10 - UA30 - James Bostic runs 1 yard at left end. Michael Rogers stops.

2nd and 9 - UA29 - Stan White pass incomplete to Thomas Bailey.

3rd and 9 - UA29 - Jeremy Nunley sacks Stan White for loss of 6 yards.

4th and 15 - UA35 - Patrick Nix completes to Frank Sanders for 35-yard touchdown. (with 6:09 remaining). Scott Etheridge kicks extra point.

SCORE: Alabama 14, Auburn 12.
DRIVE: Ten plays, 73 yards, 3:33.

Bryan Karkoska kicks off. Out of bounds.

POSSESSION TO ALABAMA (with 6:09 remaining)

1st and 10 - UA35 - Chris Anderson runs 2 yards at center. Jason Miska, Mike Pina and Terry Solomon make tackle.

2nd and 8 - UA37 - Jay Barker completes pass to David Palmer. Penalty on Alabama (holding - 16 yards).

2nd and 24 - UA21 - Jay Barker incomplete to Chad Key. Penalty on Alabama (illegal shift - declined).

3rd and 24 - UA21 - Jay Barker incomplete to David Palmer. Ricardo Walker pressures.

4th and 24 - UA21 - Bryne Diehl punts 39 yards to Auburn 40. Ball is downed.

POSSESSION TO AUBURN (with 4:42 remaining)

1st and 10 - AU40 - Tony Richardson runs 4 yards up middle. Willie Gaston and Elverett Brown make tackle.

2nd and 6 - AU44 - James Bostic runs 24 yards at left guard. Antonio Langham stops.

1st and 10 - UA32 - Patrick Nix completes 6-yard pass to Frank Sanders. Antonio Langham makes tackle.

2nd and 4 - UA26 - Tony Richardson runs 2 yards at right guard. Sam Shade and Lemanski Hall make stop.

3rd and 2 - UA24 - Reid McMilion runs 3 yards at center. Jeremy Nunley and Willie Gaston make tackle.

1st and 10 - UA21 - James Bostic runs 13 yards around left end. Tackled by Willie Gaston.

1st and G - UA8 - Jeremy Nunley and Michael Rogers stack James Bostic for 4-yard loss.

2nd and G - UA12 - Reid McMilion runs 1 yard at left guard. Jeremy Nunley makes tackle. End of quarter.

SCORE: Alabama 14, Auburn 12.

FOURTH QUARTER

3rd and G - UA11 - James Bostic runs 2 yards at left tackle. Stopped by Lemanski Hall.

4th and G - UA9 - Scott Etheridge kicks 26-yard field goal (with 14:14 remaining).

SCORE: Auburn 15, Alabama 14
DRIVE: Ten plays, 51 yards, 5:28.
Bryan Karkoska kicks off to David Palmer at Alabama 5. Palmer returns 17 yards and is stopped by Mike Pina and Kelsey Crook.

POSSESSION TO ALABAMA (with 14:06 remaining)

1st and 10 - UA22 - Jay Barker completes 5-yard pass to Kevin Lee. Chris Shelling and Mike Pina make tackle.

2nd and 5 - UA27 - Chris Anderson runs 3 yards up middle. Ricardo Walker and Randy Hart make tackle.

3rd and 2 - UA30 - Jay Barker's pass is intercepted by Derrick Robinson at the Auburn 41. Robinson returns 17 yards. Penalty on Auburn (personal foul - 15 yards).

POSSESSION TO AUBURN (with 12:54 remaining)

1st and 10 - AU44 - James Bostic runs 4 yards at left tackle. Jeremy Nunley tackles.

2nd and 6 - AU48 - Tony Richardson runs 1 yard at center. Michael Rogers and John Walters make tackle.

3rd and 5 - AU49 - James Bostic runs 2 yards at left tackle. Jeremy Nunley and Chris Donnelly make tackle.

4th and 3 - UA49 - Terry Daniel punts 49 yards to the endzone. Touchback.

POSSESSION TO ALABAMA (with 10:50 remaining)

1st and 10 - UA20 - Sherman Williams runs 4 yards at left end. Tackled by Brian Robinson.

2nd and 6 - UA24 - Sherman Williams runs 3 yards at right guard. Terry Solomon and Mike Pina make stop.

3rd and 3 - UA27 - Sherman Williams runs 2 yards at right end. Jason Miska tackles.

4th and 1 - UA29 - Tarrant Lynch runs at center. No gain.

POSSESSION TO AUBURN (with 8:55 remaining)

1st and 10 - UA29 - James Bostic runs at right end. No gain. Stopped by Willie Gaston and Lemanski Hall.

2nd and 10 - UA29 - Patrick Nix completes pass to Tony Richardson for 9 yards. John Walters makes tackle.

3rd and 1 - UA20 - Patrick Nix keeps for 1 yard up middle. Elverett Brown makes stop.

1st and 10 - UA19 - Tony Richardson runs 3 yards at left end. John Walters and Willie Gaston make tackle.

2nd and 7 - UA16 - James Bostic runs 14 yards at right end. Tackled by Willie Gaston.

1st and G - UA2 - James Bostic runs wide right and loses 6 yards. Stopped by John Walters.

2nd and G - UA8 - James Bostic runs up middle for 3 yards. Tackled by Jeremy Nunley.

3rd and G - UA5 - Tony Richardson runs 4 yards up middle.

4th and G - UA1 - Scott Etheridge 18-yard field goal attempt is botched. Sean Carder carries for no gain.

POSSESSION TO ALABAMA (with 3:51 remaining)

1st and 10 - UA1 - Jay Barker incomplete pass to Chad Key.

2nd and 10 - UA1 - Jay Barker completes 23-yard pass to David Palmer. Tackle by Chris Shelling.

1st and 10 - UA24 - Jay Barker incomplete to David Palmer. Penalty on Auburn (pass interference - 12 yards).

1st and 10 - UA36 - Tarrant Lynch runs at center. No gain. Stopped by Jason Miska.

2nd and 10 - UA36 - Jay Barker incomplete to David Palmer.

3rd and 10 - UA36 - Jay Barker incomplete to Chris Anderson. Jason Miska pressures.

4th and 10 - UA36 - Jay Barker's pass intercepted by Dell McGee at Auburn 30. No return.

POSSESSION TO AUBURN (with 2:32 remaining)

1st and 10 - AU30 - James Bostic runs 70 yards for touchdown (with 2:19 remaining).
Scott Etheridge kicks extra point.

SCORE: Auburn 22, Alabama 14.
DRIVE: One play, 70 yards, 0:13

Bryan Karkoska kicks off to David Palmer at Alabama 5. Palmer returns 22 yards. Stopped by Carlos Thornton.

POSSESSION TO ALABAMA (with 2:12 remaining)

1st and 10 - UA27 - Jay Barker pass incomplete to Toderick Malone.

2nd and 10 - UA27 - Jay Barker sacked for 1-yard loss by Willie Whitehead and Damon Primus.

3rd and 11 - UA26 - Jay Barker completes 15-yard pass to Chad Key.

1st and 10 - UA41 - Jay Barker pass incomplete. Barker down with injury.

2nd and 10 - UA41 - Brian Burgdorf completes pass to Toderick Malone. Penalty on Alabama (illegal motion - 5 yards).

2nd and 15 - UA36 - Brian Burgdorf sacked by Anthony Harris for 5-yard loss.

3rd and 20 - UA31 - Brian Burgdorf incomplete to David Palmer.

4th and 20 - UA31 - Brian Burgdorf completes 27-yard pass to Chris Anderson.

1st and 10 - UA42 - Brian Burgdorf incomplete to David Palmer.

2nd and 10 - UA42 - Jason Miska sacks Brian Burgdorf for 7-yard loss.

3rd and 17 - UA49 - Brian Burgdorf incomplete to Toderick Malone.

4th and 17 - UA49 - Brian Burgdorf incomplete to Toderick Malone.

POSSESSION TO AUBURN (with 0:21 remaining)

1st and 10 - AU49 - Patrick Nix drops to his knee. Time runs out.

FINAL SCORE:
Auburn 22, Alabama 14.

Coach Terry Bowden takes the reins as head football coach at Auburn University.
Bernard Troncale photo

Chapter Two

Bowden Takes The Helm

In a whirlwind two days, Bowden was Tigers' man

By Wayne Martin

AUBURN, December 20, 1992—Goodbyes to the old usually come before hellos to the new.

When someone moves on to a greater challenge, it's normal to first bid farewell to those who have been a part of the challenge just met. But for former Samford University football coach Terry Bowden, things were turned upside-down during a whirlwind two days that marked the end of Auburn's search for a replacement for coach Pat Dye, and the naming of Bowden to the post.

So Friday morning at 7:30, Bowden started saying his goodbyes at Samford, 17 hours after he had said hello to the Auburn Tigers family.

The turnaround was made necessary because even Bowden didn't know for sure he was the new coach until he arrived at Auburn Thursday morning.

"I told no one," he said, "because I didn't know myself. The people at Auburn called me and asked me if I could come prepared to spend the day, and if I would bring my wife. Of course, I had a pretty good idea. I didn't expect to get down there and have two coaches' wives sitting out in the foyer."

Bowden did manage to locate Samford president Dr. Thomas Corts, in the barber shop. "I got him out of the barber chair," Bowden said. "We had talked before, and I told him I felt I had a chance, so he wasn't totally surprised."

Bowden declines to talk about the process. "Some people fell you are being deceptive, but in situations like this people's jobs are at stake,"

Auburn President William Muse introduces Bowden to the media and college community.
Bernard Troncale photo

Bowden said. "Some of those candidates were afraid to go back and tell their presidents. You have to protect the people who are involved on both sides of the selection process."

He did say that his hiring by Auburn was very much like his hiring at Samford. The hiring six years ago at Samford involved the coach and the president. "That's pretty much the way it was at Auburn," he said. "My discussions were basically with two people (Auburn president William Muse and athletic director Mike Lude)."

Auburn was an offer the 36-year-old Bowden couldn't refuse. His timetable called for building Samford until the right offer came along. "I've had a lot of people talk to me over the years, officially and unofficially," he said. "I've been offered some really top Division I-AA jobs, but I chose to stay at Samford.

"There are some I-A jobs that have been available, and there are some that I talked to who didn't offer, and I'm glad. Some of them I may have taken, and it would have been a mistake."

A constant in Bowden's decision-making process has been conversations with his dad,

Florida State head coach Bobby Bowden. But was this one such a top-of-the-line job that he needed no advice?

"I needed it more on this one than any other," Terry said. "I talked to him (Bobby) first and last."

Bowden is one of just a few coaches who have moved up form a lower football classification to a head job at a Division I-A school. The normal move is from a I-A staff. And some point out that the name Bowden opened doors.

"When I was 26, I was the youngest head (college) coach in the country (at Salem College)," he said, "and I got the job because my name is Bowden. But I won. Four years later I went to Samford, and my name was still Bowden, and I won.

"Maybe being a Bowden was a factor at Auburn. If so, I apologize. I'll always be a Bowden. I'm proud of my name and my family. But if I don't win, it will make no difference what my name is."

"Terry is in control of his career," said Samford linebacker coach Tony Ierulli, who has been with him since his Salem days. "What he has achieved hasn't been because of family, it has been because of hard work. He is totally committed as a coach, he is articulate, he has outstanding organizational skills and he has a plan for success.

"If Terry Bowden wasn't coaching, he'd have been one of the country's youngest CEOs at a major company."

There was pride at Samford Thursday. "We pride ourselves at Samford on grooming and developing," said Corts. "We groomed and developed another outstanding Division I coach."

But there was more than just a little concern among the coaching family. Handshakes of congratulations were offered Friday morning, early, before Bowden sat down behind closed doors with his old staff.

"I'll admit it," said assistant Clint Conque, "I didn't sleep well last night. I'd love to got to Auburn with him, but we just don't know."

"I believe I can coach on this (I-A) level," Bowden said. "I believe Auburn hired the best man

for the job. I wouldn't be doing the job justice if I hired the second best staff. Hiring the best staff is the first priority."

And Bowden said he'll do that "like anybody else would. They (Auburn) have a staff," he said, "and I have a staff. But you add nine and six and that's 15. Some of mine may not want to go, some down there may not want to stay.

"But I have complete freedom to hire those I want to hire from here or there, or from outside."

Among the coaches who reportedly had been considered for the Auburn job were Dick Sheridan of North Carolina State, Pat Sullivan of TCU and Bill Lewis of Georgia Tech. Each withdrew his name from consideration for the AU post in published reports on Thursday, the day Bowden was hired.

"I wasn't on the inside in this situation, but I know the procedure," Bowden said. "Normally, when a decision is made, those coaches who had

Bowden meets his squad at spring practice and points them toward the future.
Mark Almond photo

Bowden and brilliant defensive coach Wayne Hall share a moment during spring moment.
Mark Almond photo

days. "I really hate that," Bowden said. "I missed them by one day."

And as the process ended at Auburn, it began at Samford. Among those expected to be considered are Southern Mississippi assistant Jeff Bowden, who is Terry's brother, and Samford assistants Bob Stinchcomb and Jack Hines.

Bowden becomes 'Auburn's coach for the future'

By Kevin Scarbinsky

AUBURN, December 18, 1992—If Terry Bowden has his way, Auburn University will not have to hire another head football coach for another three decades.

"I need to be here till I'm about 68 and win eight games a year," Bowden said Thursday (Dec. 17, 1992) after being named the 23rd coach in Auburn history. "That'll give me 324 wins."

If his math was off, his confidence and his enthusiasm hit the bulls eye with the Auburn search committee looking for a successor to Pat Dye. Eight wins a year for 33 years plus the 65 wins he already owns from six seasons at Samford University and three seasons at Salem College would give the 36-year-old Bowden 329 career wins, a half-dozen more than one Paul "Bear" Bryant.

"That's where dreams come from," Bowden said. "You don't just wander your way to the top of the mountain."

To start, Bowden will operate under a five-year contract with a base salary of $90,000 a year that will be supplemented by outside income from such sources as radio and television shows and a shoe contract. All of those terms had not been finalized by the time Bowden was introduced here Thursday afternoon, but university president William Muse said he expected the contract to be signed today.

"Terry Bowden is the coach of the future," Muse said. "He's Auburn's coach for the future."

If is sounded brash for a 36-year-old who has never been a head coach at the Division I-A level to

been considered are given the courtesy of withdrawing their names. It would seem odd that the other candidates are pulled out within a day or two of each other, had they not known a decision had been made."

The speed with which things unfolded made it possible for Bowden to meet with his players at Samford. Most had already left for Christmas holi-

An anxious Terry Bowden talks with his players as they wait to run on the field to begin the 1993 season.

refer to Bryant, the winningest I-A coach in history, it sounded like a breath of fresh air to an Auburn program in the midst of a 15-month dark cloud seeded by allegations, and the program likely will not be sentenced by the NCAA until spring.

That cloud did not deter Bowden, who Muse said was one of seven candidates interviewed by the university's search committee from Saturday (Dec. 12) through Monday (Dec. 14). The other candidates interviewed included longtime Auburn assistant Wayne Hall, the only assistant coach interviewed, and head coaches Dick Sheridan of North Carolina State, Pat Sullivan of Texas Christian and Bill Lewis of Georgia Tech. Athletic director Mike Lude said despite rampant speculation, Miami coach Dennis Erickson was not interviewed for the job.

"We knew a lot about all the candidates we interviewed before we talked to them," Muse said.

"We knew Bowden met the criteria (which included a Southern background). We didn't know a lot about his personal characteristics. That all came through strongly in the interview. Those are the things that really set him apart. His enthusiasm, his desire to be successful, his understanding of the game. He's a real motivator."

Bobby Lowder, a member of the Auburn board of trustees who served on the search committee, compared Bowden's "intensity" and "energy" during his interview with that of Dye during his interview when he got the job before the 1991 season.

Bowden was interviewed Monday, and one member of the search committee said his interview lasted longer than any of the other candidates.

"After we completed all the interviews Monday evening," Muse said, "he was the leading candidate."

Muse said he called Bowden Tuesday to ask

The sideline general directs traffic during an early season game.

direction if I were not the best man for the job."

Lude said he called Sullivan and Sheridan and the other coaches who were interviewed to let them know Wednesday that Auburn had made a decision. Sullivan, Sheridan and Georgia Tech's Bill Lewis all announced Wednesday that they had withdrawn their names from consideration.

"Before we ever had anybody decide they were not going to pursue the job," Lude said, "Terry Bowden was the first choice."

Before Auburn slumped to 5-6 and 5-5-1 records the past two years, before the program was hit with Ramsey's allegations, Bowden dreamed of coaching at Auburn just as his father had. Bobby Bowden, the Birmingham native and longtime Florida State head coach, called the Auburn job, "one of the best jobs in the country."

Terry Bowden said he talked to his father after his initial interview with the Auburn search committee.

"If we've sat down once, we've sat down 100 times as a family and said, 'What are the jobs you could stay at for the rest of your life?' Auburn was one of them," Terry said.

"I asked him a couple of days ago and he said, 'If they call back, make sure that's what you want to do because you'll never leave.'"

Bowden said he did not apply for the Auburn job, a Bobby Bowden rule of thumb in all coaching searches, and was not contacted by Auburn until a week ago.

"I felt in my heart I would be at an Auburn or a Florida State at some time in my career," Terry Bowden said. "Ten years from now I wouldn't have been too old. But I told them in my interview, by that time I'll probably be coaching one of the teams you play against."

Instead he'll be coaching Auburn next season against the Samford team he left to take this job.

He said his first priority will be recruiting. He said his second priority will be hiring a staff, with the stickiest question whether to retain his older

him to come back for a second interview, which took place Thursday morning, and afterward Muse offered the job and Bowden accepted. Muse said no one else was offered the job, and he said Bowden was the committee's first choice.

"They better not have hired me if I wasn't," Bowden said. "I believe I am the best candidate for the job. I believe Auburn would not have gone this brother Tommy, who was Dye's offensive coordinator the past two years. Bowden said will serve as his own offensive coordinator as he did at Samford and Salem.

He said his annual priority, during an anticipated NCAA probation period and beyond for what he hopes will be three decades, will be to beat Alabama.

"I will probably not be accepted here until I beat Alabama," Bowden said. "I know that. That's the way it is and that's the way it should be."

At age 37, Bowden ready for big time

By Jimmy Bryan

AUBURN, March 28, 1993—When Terry Bowden walked onto the field as head coach at Division III Salem College in 1983, he knew he was ready. He was 27 years old. When he became head coach at Samford University in 1988, leading the school from Division III to Division I-AA, he knew he was ready. He was 30 years old.

As the new head coach at Division I Auburn University this year, he knows he is ready for the big time. He is now 37 years

old.

Bowden has climbed to the top remarkably quick, and Thursday he begins proving he belongs there. He carries his first Auburn team onto the field for the beginning of spring practice.

Pressure?

"There is pressure everywhere," Bowden said. "If you don't win, you get fired. I got the Salem job because the coach before me didn't win. Samford fired a good ol' Baptist coach because he didn't win."When the Auburn job came open I was ready because my little program was winning. Whatever job you get, you better do it better than anybody else. When they call your number, you better be ready. When Auburn called mine, I was ready.

"If I don't win, I'll be fired at Auburn. The support I've received at Auburn has been overwhelming, but I've got to win some games before Auburn people hang their hat on me.

"I am Samford's man. I know that. But I won't

An intense Bowden had anxious moments during the 1993 Florida game, his biggest victory to that date.
Steve Barnette photo

be Auburn's man until I get out there, win some games and beat the cross-state rival."

Bowden begins the process of returning to Auburn to prominence after back-to-back seasons of 5-6 and 5-5-1. He welcomes a nucleus of 16 starters on offense and defense, five specialists and 56 lettermen.

Auburn fans will recognize tight end Andy Fuller, tackle Wayne Gandy, guards Shannon Roubique and Anthony Redmond, center Greg Thompson, wide receivers Orlando Parker and Thomas Bailey, quarterback Stan White, tailback James Bostic and fullback Tony Richardson as offensive starters.

Also, end Willie Whitehead, tackle Damon Primus, cornerbacks Calvin Jackson and Fred Smith and safeties Otis Mounds and Chris Shelling return on defense.

Place-kicker Scott Etheridge, punter Terry Daniel, snapper Brian Brinsfield, holder Clay Helton and kickoff man Bryan Karkoska are backs as well.

"It's a new coaching regime," Bowden said, "but we think we have incumbent starters. A lot of the coaches are still here, so there's no reason to go back to zero. But everybody has an equal chance.

"We'll change many things on offense, and I'll be right in the middle of that. We are not going to be very complex or diversified this spring. We will get down to the basics. We'll change the wording and coding systems, but we won't change how to stick a headgear in somebody's chest and block.

"Defensively, I'll defer to Coach (Wayne) Hall (retained as assistant head coach and defensive coordinator). Auburn has had some of the best defensive teams in the conference since he has been here, and that's the kind of defense we want every year.

"We will spend a lot of time on the kicking

A visibly drained Coach Bowden meets with the press after the Florida game to discuss the importance of that victory.
Steve Barnette photo

game and have it nailed down by the end of spring. We return two of the top kickers in the conference. We can have a great kicking game. We are going to do everything we can to make sure we don't lose the kicking game."

Bowden doesn't expect a finished product when spring practice ends April 24.

"We won't be ready for the first game coming out of the spring," he said. "We may not look like somebody wants us to, but we will be ready for two-a-days in August."

Bowden said he expects three-year starting quarterback Stan White to fit the new offense—a basic two-back, two-wideouts set.

"Stan's physical talent and ability fits right into our offense," he added. "So does Patrick Nix, and on down the line. What you can't know about are the intangibles — throwing the ball where it's supposed to be, holding the ball when receivers are covered, making the handoff properly.

"Stan should be a full go for practice. He had left shoulder surgery. He doesn't throw with his left hand. We probably won't let him get hit, but we can find out what we need to know."

To nail it down, Bowden said his three major priorities are:

• Establish a good relationship with the players — what the coaches expect from them and what the players can expect from the coaches.

• "Get our fundamental schemes in. We'll be doing things differently on both offense and defense and (both) need to be fundamentally sound.

• "Find the top 11 on offense and top 11 on defense.

The Tigers will work primarily on Mondays, Wednesdays, Fridays and Saturdays but will have leeway to change. The A-Day game is scheduled for April 24.

"People say they bet I can't wait for next season," Bowden said. "Yes, I can wait for next season. I want every single day available to get ready for Sept. 2 and Ole Miss."

Bowden no stranger to pressure

By Clyde Bolton

AUBURN, Sunday, Jan. 17, 1993—Terry Bowden pointed me to an expansive couch in his office. "I can't sit there," he said, taking a chair. "My feet won't touch the floor."

How tall is Bowden? "I'm 5-6," he said, "or 5-9 if you read the program from when I played football.

"Dad and I may not be the only father-son in (NCAA Division) I-A, but we must be the shortest. He's 5-8."

On the coffee table between us are two books. One was about Bobby Bowden, Saint Bobby and the Barbarians. The other was Pat Dye's autobiography, In the Arena.

Terry Bowden, as Auburn's new football coach, will be measured against these two men, his father and his predecessor. Pressure?

Bowden chose his words carefully. "I don't want to make it sound like there's not a lot of pressure," he said, "but there always has been.

"You may say, 'If you don't win at Auburn, they'll fire you.

"But if you don't win at Samford, you don't get to Auburn. If you don't win at Salem, you don't get to Samford."

Bowden grimaced. "In my first year as a head coach I was 0-and-7 at Salem and 26 years old and nobody to help me. Now, that was a lot of pressure."

TO THE RESCUE

Terry Bowden is a Rescue 911 type. In 1983 he took over a Salem team that hadn't won a game the season before, and in 1984 his club went 8-3 and reached the Division III playoffs. In 1987 he became head coach of the Samford Bulldogs, who had won just six games in three years. His first squad did 9-1, and he was named national Co-Coach of the Year. In 1988 Samford made the huge leap to I-AA. By 1991 the Bulldogs were going 12-2 and participating in the playoffs.

Auburn's program isn't a wreck, but it is in need of repair, and the mess with the NCAA hangs like a Damocles sword. Thirty-six-year old Terry Bowden was the surprise choice to be the mechanic.

He brings a fine sense of humor to the post. "I'm two years older than Vince Dooley was when he got the job at Georgia," he approached the subject of his age. "But, then, I'm about the same age as Mike Archer." Archer, of course, was the young coach whom LSU canned.

Bowden hasn't lived a lot of years, but he has spent them all with a football under his arm or in his crib. "I've been around long enough to know whether a school has what it takes to win," he said, mentioning condition, facilities, etc. "Auburn has what it takes. We're not a have-not."

It's just a matter of applying the assets. "The secret of winning football games is that there is no secret," Bowden said. "Auburn should be able to develop a top, top program."

He added: "I'm confident. If it can be done I can do it."

Bowden doesn't pussyfoot around the core issue. "You've got to beat Alabama in the first three or four years." Otherwise, he said, the fans' confidence in the coach erodes.

The Tigers of 1992 "weren't that bad on defense," Bowden said. He will tell the defensive coaches to keep on doing what they've been doing.

"There were a lot of reasons Auburn didn't have good offensive results," he added, refusing to elaborate.

CONFIDENCE NEEDED

The Tigers — particularly the offense — need a confidence implant. "You lose five games for two straight seasons, your confidence is down," Bowden said. "That doesn't take a rocket scientist."

But the man who had confidence enough to go from 0-7 at Salem to head man at Auburn is a football coach, not a psychiatrist. "If your confidence is shaken, it's understandable," he said. "If it can't be restored, that's intolerable. If somebody has had so many losses they can't pull it out, we'll have to find somebody else."

Bowden settles in at Auburn

By Clyde Bolton

AUBURN, Wednesday, March 24, 1993—You can be certain folks from the national newspapers and TV networks will be drinking lemonade at Toomer's Corner, just as John Heisman used to, this football season.

Terry Bowden's debut as Auburn's head coach is a natural as national stories go: The son of famous coach Bobby Bowden gets his chance at the big time, striding through the wreckage wrought by Eric Ramsey's tapes.

Bowden is settling in, learning where all the closets and light switches are. "The first thing you've got to learn is what not to do," Bowden reflected in his monstrous office. (I've hit 7-irons that wouldn't have reached from wall to wall.) "You want to be available to everybody and make a good impression—press, staff, alumni. You come in wanting to be all things to all people—but I'm learning that you can't."

DOUBLE TIME

Bowden and wife Shyrl and their three daughters have moved into Sewell Hall, the athletic dorm, while they make arrangements for permanent housing, just as Pat and Sue Dye once did.

"My children are in there running around and having a great time with the players," he said. "By being in there, I'm probably doubling or tripling the time I have with the athletes."

Bowden's first A-Day game will be April 24, and he hopes that will end spring drills. "We'll try to get it all in before A-Day," he said. "The kids kinda quit playing after A-Day. They feel like football is over."

Bowden is installing his offense, so the going will be slow at first. "We won't be able to do much scrimmaging the first week because we'll be learning the system," he said. "This will be their third change offensively in about four years, so it will mean spring ball will come a little slower."

Bowden runs a "tight end, two-back offense" that features adaptability. "It's one we can grow with," he said. In his offense, "there can be a toss sweep every time or a pass every time. It's an offense that's adjustable to everything we'll do in the future."

Bowden poses with his players before the game; Todd Boland (52), Anthony Redmond (65), Greg Thompson (54), Terry Daniel (36), Scott Etheridge (43).

OFFENSE AND DEFENSE

Spring practice will reveal Auburn's offensive capabilities and lack of same, and the coaches will work from there. Last year the Tigers were decent on defense, erratic on offense.

It will be interesting to see exactly what path Auburn does follow when it has the ball. Alabama's success last season, keyed to defense, made a huge impression on Bowden. Twice he has mentioned it to me.

He said wide-open offense is "in my blood," but he noted: "Alabama has taught us all a lesson — us fancy offensive coaches especially. You win on defense and don't lose on offense."

Wide-open offense got a boost when the NCAA approved moving the hash marks nearer the center of the field. Last season they were 53 feet, 4 inches from the sidelines. This year they will be 60 feet. In the pros, they are 70 feet, 9 inches.

"You can throw better with the ball nearer the middle of the field," Bowden said. "The defense can use the boundary as a defensive man, but not when the hash marks are near the middle. It's going to cause everybody to do some thinking about offense during the spring."

These are interesting times at Auburn. A rehabilitator is at the wheel. In 1983 Bowden took over a Salem club that hadn't won a game, and in two seasons it was in the playoffs. In 1987 he inherited a Samford team that had won just six games in three years, and he immediately won nine. Following his adventures at Auburn will be more fun than keeping up with a soap opera.

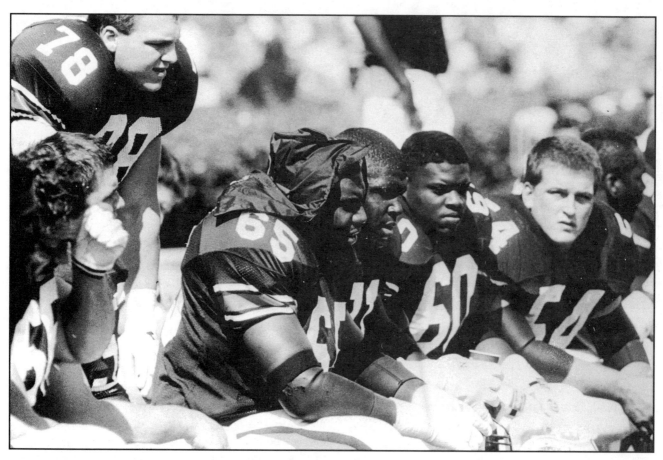

Auburn offensive linemen get a breather during the Auburn/Alabama game; from left to right, Brian Osborn (78), Anthony Redmond (65), Willie Anderson (71), Leonard Thomas (60), and Greg Thompson (54).
Steve Barnette photo

Chapter Three

The Season

Bowden expresses doubts

Neal Sims, News staff writer

Average Auburn. That's Terry Bowden's opinion of his first football team as the Tigers' new head coach.

Now, what Bowden wants this year is a take-it-down-to-the-wire Auburn, a team that brings its games into the final minutes with a shot at winning. Success in enough of those situations is the key to the season.

"I am not taking over an Auburn team that is not competitive," Bowden told the Kickoff '93 gathering here for Southeastern Conference Media Days. "If I had a label for the team that I inherited, it is one that I don't like very much. We are an av-

erage football team. That's where we start. We have got to play with that in mind.

"It gets me," Bowden said later Tuesday, "but it's says exactly where we are. I'd rather be terrible or better, so bad that you have to do something different. It's just where we stand."

Still, Bowden said a winning season for the Tigers is realistic after 5-6 and 5-5-1 records in former coach Pat Dye's final two years. The difference will be winning some of those close ones that got away at the end.

"If we can play at last year's level and have the same type of success, we're that close," said Bowden. "We're one tie away. If we can play at our best, we're talking about some tight, tight ballgames."

Even with an average team in a tough league, said Bowden, "You can still be in ballgames and win ballgames if you play with the philosophy that you're going to take it down to the wire.

"All games are 60 minutes, but a few of them

Bowden's motto for his Auburn football team is AttitUde as it says on the scoreboard in the background. It is a motto adopted by the fans as well.
Bernard Troncale photo

are determined in the last couple of minutes. If we have a better football season, it will be because of games that we win in the last minute. We've got to be ready to take our victories however we can."

One of the youngest coaches in major college football, Bowden finds himself in one of the nation's strongest conferences, and in the SEC West Division going up against coaches like Alabama's Gene Stallings, Arkansas' Danny Ford and Mississippi State's Jackie Sherrill. "The SEC right now is at a time when it is as strong as it's been in a long while," said Bowden.

Six league teams played in bowl games last season, and Auburn plays five of them including four winners, national champion Alabama, Florida, Georgia and Ole Miss.

"When you're an average football team," said Bowden, "there is no tendency to look beyond any game.

"We're at a position right now in our program where we need to focus on beating Ole Miss (in the season opener Sept. 2). We don't need to go look across the state right now and compare everything we do with where they are. We need to focus on being better than we were last year."

Senior quarterback Stan White views his final season at Auburn the same way. "Wins and losses, checking the record," said White. "If we were to go out and have a considerably better year than the last couple of years, know that we were in every game, know we had a chance to win every game and we won some we weren't supposed to win, that would be a successful season to me." Bowden reiterated that White holds down the starting spot at quarterback as the coach touched on a number of other topics during the media gathering.

On White, Bowden said, "Stan White is the No. 1 quarterback based on what he showed me in spring practice in head-to-head competition with other quarterbacks. I anticipate him entering the season as the No. 1 quarterback. Right now, he's a little bit better than Patrick Nix.

"Stan White is a good enough quarterback to play foot ball at Auburn and be able to run our offense. He has the tools necessary for us to have a good offense.

"We may have to be careful about what we ask our quarterback to do because of the talent on our team. If we don't catch it consistently, maybe we shouldn't be throwing it so much. Maybe we should go out there and do the best we can running the football." On Steve Davis, the nation's No. 1 prospect in 1991, now available after sitting out last season to become academically eligible, Bowden said he'll have to work to find a place in an Auburn backfield that includes All SEC tailback James Bostic.

"James Bostic is going to play tailback," said Bowden. "I'm a big James Bostic fan. He does not think for a second that Steve Davis is going to get a rip at tailback unless it's to rest him. He is our tailback. We'll let that develop."

On the pending announcement from the NCAA about possible sanctions against Auburn, Bowden said, "I haven't seen a whole lot of reaction from the players. It's on all of the fans' minds. It's the talk on the street. Whether you're for us or against us, it's interesting conversation. But for the players, it's not something you sense is in their minds.

"To be honest with you," Bowden added, "our goals are so clearly defined this year, so short-term and identifiable, that there is nothing the NCAA can do to keep us from reaching our goals. I don't believe the NCAA decision will have near the impact on our team that might be suspected."

"*Attitude*" is Auburn motto for season

Neal Sims, News staff writer

AUBURN—This will be their motto, one word for the Auburn Tigers to live and play by in 1993: *Attitude.*

Make that attitude with a capital "AU," as in "AttitUde."

That was the message new Auburn football coach Terry Bowden delivered to his players Wednesday night in a motivational meeting on the eve of today's first full-squad workouts of the pre-season.

Bowden wore the motto on his orange and blue shirt button and preached the message in his talk. It will be a slogan, a reminder that the Tigers will see and hear frequently this year.

"I'm trying to express in words what I'm hoping

our players are thinking about," said Bowden. "I'm looking for one word, one phrase that sums up our thoughts."

Bowden has had his mottos with other teams in other places. One was "TNT" or Today, Not Tomorrow. Last year at Samford, it was "STP" or Something To Prove.

"Here," Bowden said, "we've got to look at it differently. We've got to go from where we've been the last couple of years to that next level. We've got to focus on what it's going to take to get from being an average football team. We have to look in the mirror and say we've just been average. That's the type of motivation we'll have. We're trying to work our way up."

In his "attitude session" with the team, Bowden put the focus on "what we want to do and how we are going to go about doing it."

"These are our goals," he added. "This is how we're going to reach them. The idea is to touch base with everybody in that room. We'll talk about the role of the backup, the role of the starter, the role of the coaches.

"You don't just wind up at the top of the mountain. You have to have a plan to get there."

While Bowden didn't say it, some Auburn followers figure that attitude, or lack of same, may have been at the root of some of the Tigers' losses the past two seasons, when the teams were beset by distractions ranging from an NCAA investigation to a coach under attack.

Bowden, assessing the Tigers talent, did point to some games last season—a loss to Georgia when the Tigers failed to get off a play near the goal line in the final seconds; a loss to Mississippi State on a punt return for a touchdown; and a loss to Alabama after playing the national champion to a scoreless tie for a half.

"The talent level is enough to be competitive and win in the SEC," he said. "That doesn't mean that we're going to be a contender for the conference championship, but I don't think we'll walk into a majority of our games and not be able to compete.

"We don't have people like Auburn had in 1987 or '88 or '89, but compared to most of our SEC opponents, we stand up pretty well. We showed we were competitive with most of these teams last year."

Now that the varsity has joined the freshmen on the practice field, the Tigers will work in shorts and helmets for three days, as required by NCAA rules. They'll go to pads and hitting next week, with a full scrimmage per haps as early as next

Auburn receiver Thomas Bailey stretches during preseason drills.
Mark Almond photo

planned for noon, with another practice scheduled from 5:30 to 8 p.m.

"There are so many things to do," said Bowden. "Check our schedule. We've got every minute planned. There is so much work and so many meetings."

The Tigers will work on fundamentals and schemes the first week or so, then turn their attention to Ole Miss, the opponent for the opening game Sept. 2, a Thursday night televised contest on ESPN.

"We only got so far in our preparations during the spring," said Bowden, who began work putting in a new offense then. "We've got to get fundamentally sound first. From an offensive standpoint, we may have to do that more before getting into a game plan.

"If you can't execute something, then don't do it. If we cannot do certain things, then we won't try to do it in the first game. The offense has the capability of a four-wide offense. But if we've got only two out there who've proven they can play, there's no reason to put that phase in. You've got to look at your talent and see where it leads you and see if it allows you to do those things."

Bowden said his freshmen and other newcomers will get a hard look right away.

"If a freshman goes out there and shows me he can jump right up and play, he's going to get some repetitions," said Bowden. "We always look at freshmen

Wednesday.

The freshmen already have worked out three days. They took Wednesday afternoon off. The varsity reported in Tuesday night and took physicals and conditioning tests Wednesday.

On most days, the Tigers will get 5 a.m. wake-up calls and hit the practice field by 6 a.m. for a two-hour session. Another one-hour workout is

early. We've seen our varsity in the spring. We've seen all the guys who are second and third-team.

"We're going to look at our freshmen immediately. We're going to give them a shot immediately in scrimmages. Those second and third-teamers may have to watch from the sidelines. They had their chance to be first-team in the spring.

"Now if those freshmen don't seem to be mature enough or quite ready, we'll go back to those other guys and get them ready. All that should not take away from first-team work."

Fall drills begin at AU

Neal Sims News staff writer

AUBURN—For now, it's mostly flexing and calisthenics, throw and catch and running drills. But full-squad football practice is under way at Auburn, where the real work will begin next week.

The varsity joined the freshmen and other newcomers on the practice field Thursday, first at 5:45 a.m. and again at 5:30 p.m., as two-a-day work sessions began for the entire team. The newcomers had been working since Sunday.

"It was a good first day," said new Auburn head coach Terry Bowden. "We are just trying to get everybody back in the feel of things. I was pleased with the attitude and willingness to work.

"This group has come back in as good a condition as any group I've ever coached," Bowden added. "They want to get better and establish good, winning habits."

The return of the varsity gives Bowden a first look at some players who missed spring football with injuries. Most notable are linebacker Carlos

Stan White (11) and Patrick Nix (10) competed during preseason drills for the starting quarterback position.
Mark Almond photo

Thornton and fullback Reid McMilion.

Bowden said he was looking forward to seeing them in action when pads go on next week.

"I expect them to fight for their positions," he said. "They have to go out there and re-establish themselves as starters before they do anything else. Then, from them, you get natural leadership. I hope they can get back in that rotation."

Thornton, a 6-foot-1, 233-pound linebacker, played in nine games last year but missed spring drills with an injured shoulder. He is counted on to bolster a linebacking crew that is already thin.

That situation got even thinner Thursday, when Bowden announced after the evening practice that redshirt freshman Patrick Epkins has decided to give up football. Epkins had been listed as second on the depth chart.

"Patrick has decided that his heart was just not in football anymore," said Bowden, "and he has decided not to continue playing. His departure leaves us with one less linebacker, but somebody will step up and we will continue to go forward."

Anthony Harris, Terry Solomon and walk-on Jason Miska, who moved into position during the spring, currently are listed as the three starting linebackers. Thornton and Chris Dewberry are the top backups.

Fall practice also marks the resumption of the quarterback battle between senior Stan White and sophomore Patrick Nix. White kept his starting job during the spring, but Bowden said he'll still be watching both.

"I'm firm that Stan is No. 1 and Pat Nix is No. 2," said Bowden. "But it's close enough that both of them could lead our offense. It's close enough that there is a race going on.

"If Stan, for some reason, did not do as well, and Patrick had a great summer throwing, it could happen."

Auburn family glad it's over

Charles Hollis and Ron Ingram, News staff writers

The verdict is in and Auburn officials are relieved.

"I'm just glad it's over," said Auburn trustee and State Rep. Jack Venable, D-Tallassee. "(The waiting) is the worst part. It's like waiting for the guillotine to fall."

After Eric Ramsey's allegations of NCAA rules violations first surfaced in September 1991 and after the NCAA detailed those violations in its preliminary letter of inquiry in November 1992, the waiting finally ended this morning. The Tigers' football program was placed on two years probation, including no television appearances for one year and the reduction of scholarships.

The university made the announcement this morning.

"It's a relief to finally hear something—to finally get it over," said trustee Charles Glover of Cullman. "Maybe now we can go back to the basics, and move on." Another trustee, State Sen. Lowell Barron, D-Fyffe, expressed surprise at the penalty. "I think the penalty is much harsher than the infraction. (Notre Dame coach) Lou Holtz admitted that he gave a player $300 at Minnesota. They (the NCAA) did nothing, so I think they have used a double standard some-what." Still, Barron said he was glad to know the NCAA infractions committee had finally made a decision. "It's a blessing. I think the sentence is too tough, but we are tougher than the sentence."

Many in the Auburn family said they had grown weary of the speculation when the verdict would come down.

One of Auburn's most decorated players, 1970 Heisman Trophy winner Pat Sullivan, said "the Auburn family can finally start putting this behind them. There's no more talk about when. There's no more suspense. It's over. And Auburn people are strong. Auburn's a family that sticks together. And Auburn—the coaches, players, administration, faculty, students, everyone connected to the university—will handle it in the right way."

Sullivan was an assistant coach under Pat Dye for five seasons. He left after the '91 season to become the head coach at Texas Christian University in Dallas. He was on Dye's staff when Ramsey first made his charges of wrongdoing in the fall of '91.

"I'm close to a lot of people there, and I'm glad this is over," Sullivan said. "I love Auburn. I know they've got excellent leadership with (AU president) Dr. (William) Muse and (athletic director) Mike Lude. They'll come out of this fine."

"You don't just wind up at the top of the mountain. You have to have a plan to get there."
—Terry Bowden

Tackle Damon Primus and end Gary Walker sandwich and Ole Miss ball carrier in what turned out to be a strong defensive effort for Bowden's first venture into SEC competition.

THE FIRST WIN
Ole Miss

Terry starts a winner, salty defense hits Ole Miss

Neal Sims, News staff writer

AUBURN—This was a celebration Terry Bowden couldn't wait to begin. Three times, the new Auburn coach came off the sidelines in the closing seconds, heading for midfield, only to be waved off for the final few ticks of the clock.

Then he had it. His first major college victory in his first major college game. Auburn beat Ole Miss 16-12 Thursday night at Jordan-Hare Stadium, building a lead then holding off a late scare from the Rebels.

"Obviously, I'm elated," said Bowden, coaching his first game since coming to Auburn from Samford last winter to replace Pat Dye. "I'm thrilled to death. I'm very glad to get that first one over with.

"We've got only one down. But it's a big one because it's one we didn't get last year. If we're going to make any strides forward, you've got to beat somebody that beat you last year. We've got that done."

Victims of a 45-21 loss last year at Ole Miss, this time the Tigers came out firing before a crowd of 78,246. They drove to a score on their first possession, settling for field goal after a touchdown was called back. Auburn did get a TD after an Ole Miss fumble, and Scott Etheridge added two more field goals to give the Tigers a 16-0 lead heading into the fourth quarter.

Ole Miss made it close on two big plays, a long touchdown pass and a late punt return with less than two minutes to play, but it was not enough to take victory away from Bowden and his Tigers.

"With about five minutes left, it hit me," said Bowden. "This is sweet. Then that punt return made it a little bit harder on me. If we'd have tackled him, that game would have been over right there, I think. Then it was all the way to the last seconds until it hit me.

"The defense had to play very good," he added. It did, holding Ole Miss to 176 total yards and recording five sacks.

"The offense had to do at least what we thought we could do, and that's run with the football," said Bowden. It did, rushing for 193 yards, 138 of them from tailback James Bostic.

"And we thought we might have to win with the kicking game," he said. Etheridge's points made the difference.

"We got some points early," said Bowden. "Our defense was in control of the ballgame. (Defensive coordinator) Wayne Hall was practically writing my game plan as the game went on. It said, "Don't worry about it. Pound out some first downs. Play field position, and let our defense stay in control.' "

Ole Miss coach Billy Brewer said, "In defense of our football team, we didn't play as well as we wanted to play. We really struggled. Auburn whipped us on both lines. Then we end up with a chance to tie the ballgame and didn't come up with it. Auburn was the better team.

"They did everything we expected them do. There wasn't a thing that they did that we weren't prepared for. Sometimes we didn't do much about it."

Auburn (1-0 overall, 1-0 in the Southeastern Conference) took an early lead in the league with the Thursday night opener. Other teams won't get under way until Saturday. Ole Miss (0-1, 0-1) will have an uphill fight in the SEC West, where it finished runner-up to Alabama last season.

The Tigers stuffed the Rebels on the game's opening possession, three plays and out, a frequent result for the Ole Miss offense all night.

Barely seven minutes passed before Auburn went on the scoreboard on its first possession of Bowden's AU career. The record will show Bowden's first play call was to fullback Tony Richardson up the middle. He got 8 yards, then a toss to Bostic got 8 more.

Quarterback Stan White hit wideout Thomas Bailey with a soft-touch, over-the-middle pass for another first down at the Ole Miss 35. The Tigers converted a third-and-one to get inside the 5. Then Richardson caught what would have been a touchdown pass, but the play was called back for illegal motion on a wideout. Etheridge put Auburn up 3-0 with a 27-yard field goal.

"That first drive was critical," said Bowden. "That set the tempo. They felt they could stop us with a three-man front. We had to run the football. That drive was critical because it showed we could run if they did not put more than three linemen and three linebackers up."

Said Brewer, "It showed they weren't intimidated by our defense."

An Ole Miss interception, one of just two Auburn turnovers, stopped the Tigers' next try at Auburn's 37. Ole Miss couldn't make it pay off, though, missing a 32-yard field goal on the opening play of the second quarter.

Later, the Rebels, pinned deep by a 49-yard punt from Terry Daniel, lost the ball when Auburn linebacker Mike Pelton sacked quarterback Lawrence Adams at the Ole Miss 16. Auburn scored in four plays, two runs by Richardson and two runs by Bostic, for a 10-0 lead.

A fake reverse set up Auburn's next score. Bostic ended up with the ball, slipped in the backfield, then broke through for a 56-yard run. "I slipped down, then I hit a crease," he said. "If I hadn't slipped, it might have been a better run." As it was, he was caught from behind at the Ole Miss 5. Another critical penalty hurt the Tigers there, 15-yards on a deadball personal foul for taunting, and again they had to settle for an Etheridge field goal. His 43-yarder made it 13-0 at the half.

A 22-yard run by Bostic opened an Auburn drive early in the third quarter, leading to Etheridge's final field goal, 28 yards for a 16-0 lead.

"They looked farther," said Etheridge of his three hits. "They all went straight and high. I was pleased. This is one of the best moments I've had in Auburn in a long time.

"I had some jitters. I could tell the coaching staff was kind of nervous. We were all nervous. We've been waiting for this game for so long."

That was the end of Auburn's scoring and the start for Ole Miss.

In the fourth quarter, AU tailback Harold Morrow lost the ball near midfield on a big hit. Two plays later, Ole Miss split end Lemay Thomas got behind the Auburn secondary, and Adams hit him with a 47-yard touchdown pass. The try for two-points failed as Auburn cornerback Calvin Jackson broke up the pass, leaving the score 16-6.

Inside two minutes, Ole Miss freshman Ta'Boris Fisher took a punt, broke through several tacklers and down the sidelines for a 77-yard TD. Again, Jackson broke up the try for two.

The Rebels tried an on-sides kick, Auburn recovered and ran out the clock on the 16-12 victory.

Defense, defense, defense

Clyde Bolton, News columnist

AUBURN—When the dissection of Terry Bowden's first game as Auburn's football coach is completed, the only statistic that will matter is this one: Auburn 16 points, Mississippi 12 points.

Auburn is off the starting line and leading the SEC standings under the league's youngest coach. It would have been a shame if the weight that has been on the Tigers' shoulders—what with probation and losing games—had been compounded by a defeat Thursday night.

But a new day dawned—if, indeed, a day can dawn at night. Terry Bowden is undefeated, and the War Eagle flies down the field. How long he will be undefeated remains to be seen, but for now, enjoy.

Auburn won with a script that plays well on the other side of the state, in Tuscaloosa. Its offense was erratic, but its defense saved the bacon.

Scott Etheridge pointed out that Auburn's defense outdid one even nearer by. "Everybody was talking about the Ole Miss defense," he commented. "Coach Bowden said, 'Let's make them talk about our defense instead.' " Hall's defense

Etheridge isn't a defender. He is a wisp of a lad whose duty is to kick field goals, and from that viewpoint he paid Wayne Hall, the defensive coordinator, the most profound compliment Hall will ever receive.

"I think Coach Hall could put 11 kickers out there and turn them into a defense," he said.

Hall is a holdover from the Pat Dye regime, a man frequently mentioned as a potential major college head coach. When Bowden was named Dye's successor, everyone wondered if Auburn was big enough for both of them, but Bowden did, indeed, retain Hall.

Why? "Because of what you saw out there tonight," Bowden answered.

What we saw was Ole Miss running for 47 yards and passing for 129 yards—47 of the passing yards coming on one play. Lawrence Adams, the sophomore quarterback, was punished by onrushing Tigers.

"We knew we had to put heat on him and make him make decisions, since this was his first time," Hall said. "He made some wrong ones.

"We blitzed and faked the blitz, and he had trouble with that."

Auburn had a shutout working in the fourth period, but Ole Miss hit a 47-yard touchdown pass and returned a punt 77 yards for a TD, and suddenly the thing had become a football game.

"They had a busted assignment and a punt return, and we can't afford those mistakes down the road," Hall said.

"YOU LIKE HIM'

Why did Hall stay at Auburn when he was snubbed for the head job?

"I like the school, and I like the people. You meet the guy, and you like him," he said of Bowden.

"There was probably a little anticipation on his part and on mine, but he's easy to work for. All you can ask of a guy you work for is that he listen to you, and he does, though he may not always agree with you."

Auburn scored 5 fewer points against Ole Miss Thursday night than it did against Ole Miss last year. It won Thursday night, it lost by 24 last year. Defense is, indeed, to be desired.

Auburn's offense, though, showed the same alarming tendency to self-destruct that hobbled it in 1992. One penalty nullified a TD, another moved AU from the Ole Miss 5 back to the 20, with a field

goal resulting. An interception led to the Rebels kicking at, but missing, a field goal, and a fumble led to an Ole Miss touchdown.

But, for the moment, Terry Bowden has a better percentage as a major college coach than his dad Bobby does.

Auburn 16
Ole Miss 12

Ole Miss	0	0	0	12—12
Auburn	3	10	3	0—16

First Quarter
Aub—FG Etheridge 27
Second Quarter
Aub—Bostic 3 run (Etheridge kick)
Aub—FG—Etheridge 37
Third Quarter
Aub—FG—Etheridge 29
Fourth Quarter
Miss—Thomas 47 pass from Adams (pass failed)
Miss—Fisher 77 punt return (pass failed)
Attendance— 78,246

	Miss	Aub
First downs	8	16
Rushes-yards	30-47	56-193
Passing	129	79
Return Yards	136	8
Comp-Att-Int	8-16-0	8-18-1
Punts	10-36	7-46
Fumbles-Lost	1-1	1-1
Penalties-Yards	6-45	6-50
Time of Possession	22:47	37:13

INDIVIDUALS
OLE MISS
Rushing

Player	Att.	Yds.	TD	Long
Adams	11	-14	13	0
Veasley	5	23	9	0
Courtney	10	22	10	0
Brown	1	3	10	0
Thornton	1	1	3	0
Preston	1	1	11	0
Peters	1	1	1	0

Passing

Player	A-C-I	Yds	TD	Long
Adams	16-8-0	129	1	47

Receiving

Player	No.	Yds	TD	Long
Veasley	1	6	0	6
Woods	2	16	0	11
Preston	2	16	0	10
Thomas	2	83	1	47
Courtney	1	8	0	8

Punting

Player	No.	Yds	Avg	Long
McCardle	10	355	35.5	44

Returns

Player	Punts	Kickoff	Int.
Smith		1-9	
Woods	2-36		
Small	5-59		
Dixon			1-0
Fisher	1-77		

AUBURN
Rushing

Player	Att.	Yds.	TD	Long
White	6	-13	3	0
Richardson	14	42	8	0
Bostic	28	132	56	1
Morrow	4	22	8	0
McMillion	4	4	5	0

Passing

Player	A-C-I	Yds	TD	Long
White	18-8-1	79	0	15

Receiving

Player	No.	Yds	TD	Long
Bailey	5	53	0	13
Sanders	1	15	0	15
Dorn	1	5	0	5
Morrow	1	6	0	6

Punting

Player	No.	Yds	Avg	Long
Daniel	7	323	46.1	50

Returns

Player	Punts	Kickoff	Int.
Bailey	2-8	1-22	

DEFENSE
OLE MISS
Tackles, assists —Jackson 10-4; Lowery 7-5: Dotson 5-3; Mays 7-1; O'Malley 4-2; Brice 4-1; Ferguson 3-1; Harris 1-3; Collier 2-2; Jones 3-0; Dickson 2-0; Bowens 2-0; Iland 0-2; McGowan 2-0; Carmichael 1-0; Evans 1-0; Orr 1-1; Logan 1-0. Sacks —Abide 1. Fumbles recovered —Brice 1. Passes intercepted —Dickson 1. Passes broken up — Brice 1.

AUBURN
Tackles, assists —Harris 8-8; Miska 6-4; Robinson 6-1; Jackson 3-3; Mounds 2-3; Solomon 2-2; Primus 2-2; Whitehead 3-1; Walker 2-2; Hart 1-3; Morrow 3-1; Pina 1-1; Pelton 0-2; Miller 1-1; Shelling 0-1; Bryan 1-0; Milford 1-0. Sacks —Harris 2, Solomon. Fumbles recovered —Pelton. Passes intercepted —None. Passes broken up —Jackson 3.

AUBURN SEASON
Results (1-0)

Sept. 2		Ole Miss, Won 16-12
Sept. 11		Samford
Sept. 18		at LSU
Sept. 25		Southern Miss
Oct. 2		at Vandy
Oct. 9		Miss. State
Oct. 16		Florida
Oct. 30		at Arkansas
Nov. 6		New Mexico St.
Nov. 13		at Georgia
Nov. 20		Alabama

Defensive end Willie Whitehead manhandles Samford's quarterback. It was the way things went all game for the out-manned and out-gunned Bulldogs.
Steve Barnett

JUST A WARMUP
Samford

Tigers whip Dogs in tune-up for SEC

Neal Sims, News staff writer

AUBURN—The Auburn side wanted more from its team. The Samford side did, too.

The big-time Tigers did beat the small-college Bulldogs 35-7 Saturday night. The victory was expected. The game expected more.

A Jordan-Hare Stadium crowd of 68,936 saw these two wrap up their two-year series. The Tigers tuned up for rougher Southeastern Conference foes to come with four touchdowns in the game's first 21 minutes, two on long scoring passes, then settled back to play it out.

"It may not be as pretty as some people wanted," said Auburn coach Terry Bowden, "but it was pretty enough for me. We got ahead early. We got ahead comfortably, then kind of got sloppy. "A bigger score wouldn't have done anything for Auburn. We got a good test from Samford."

Said Samford coach Chan Gailey, "No, I don't believe in moral victories. I can't walk into any dressing room and say "good job' if we lose the football game. I can say "great effort.' I can say how proud I am of them. I can tell them I love them. But I don't believe in moral victories.

"We dropped too many passes. We had too many penalties. We turned the ball over. You can't beat Podunk U. with a performance like that."

Auburn (2-0 overall, 1-0 in the SEC) rolled up 409 yards in total offense but gave up 260 to Division I-AA Samford (1-1). Stephen Davis, making his debut at running back for the Tigers, was the game's leading rusher with 122 yards, two touchdowns and one 48-yard gainer.

The Bulldogs got 16 first downs against the Tigers but lost a fumble and had two interceptions that led to Auburn TDs.

"You've got to give Samford a lot of credit," said Bowden, who coached the Bulldogs last season when they lost to Auburn 55-0. "They did a super job of running their offense. We just had to go out there and react to it. You couldn't hardly prepare for it. That's all we were doing was trying to react to things we hadn't seen before.

"It feels a lot better being on the winning team," added Bowden.

The Tigers got to midfield on their first possession but were stopped by the Samford defense. Then the Tigers scored the next four times they had the ball.

The Bulldogs were moving on their first possession before the turnovers spoiled their early hopes. Samford got first downs on a 13-yard run by H-back Wendell Magee and a 14-yard pass from Bart Yancey to wideout Ron Green.

Then Yancey, under pressure from Auburn defensive end Willie Whitehead, threw an interception that was picked off near midfield by linebacker Anthony Harris.

Auburn quarterback Stan White quickly found tight end Derrick Dorn over the middle for a 16-yard gain to the Samford 30. Two carries by tailback James Bostic got the Tigers to the 18, then White hit wideout Frank Sanders, who scrambled in for the first score barely seven minutes into the game.

Samford began moving again. This time, an Auburn interception was wiped out by an offsides penalty, and the Bulldogs got a first down at the Tigers' 46 on a pass interference call. But after Magee made a catch for a 12-yard gain, he fumbled and Mike Pelton recovered for Auburn.

Three plays brought the Tigers back to midfield, and wide receiver Thomas Bailey took a pass from White on the sidelines around the Samford 30, slipped a tackler and scored on the 50-yard play to make it 14-0.

Davis, the acclaimed running back recruit, made his first game appearance for Auburn with 1:47 to go in the first quarter. His first carry was a

Auburn offensive lineman pushed back Samford defenders to give tailback James Bostic room to run.
Hal Yeager photo

burst though the middle, a gain of 30 yards to the Samford 26. Another newcomer, freshman tight end Jessie McCovery, caught a pass at the 15.

Davis' second carry was a 12-yard ramble to the 2, then he rammed inside close to the goal line. His fourth run was for the touchdown, and Auburn was up 21-0 with nearly 14 minutes still to play in the first half.

Samford then put up its only score of the night, set up by a 47- yard kickoff return by Marcus Durgin. The Bulldogs drove 48 yards on the Tigers in seven plays, including a first down on a fourth-and-two play from the Auburn 27. Yancey hit wideout Ron Green for the touchdown on a 24-yard pass.

The Tigers came right back to answer the Bulldogs with another bomb. This one capped a 79-yard drive in three plays, the score coming on a 53-yard pass from White to Sanders. The half ended with Auburn up 28-7.

"PLAY A LOT OF PEOPLE'

"The second half," said Bowden, "we were just looking to get a score, then play a lot of people."

In the third quarter, Samford running back Anthony Jordan tried a halfback pass, and Auburn safety Brian Robinson picked it off and returned his interception 36 yards to the Samford 13. Two runs by Davis, for 3 and 10 yards, got his second touchdown and put Auburn ahead 35-7.

Auburn went with reserves the rest of the way, as Bowden looked to build up playing depth for the rest of the season.

Quarterback Patrick Nix directed a drive to the Samford 5, the big play a 32-yard pass to wideout Tyrone Goodson to the 12. Three runs by Davis got the Tigers close, but he was stopped short on a fourth-down try from there.

Samford drove to the Auburn 10 in the second half, but Dawson Ingram missed a field goal.

Auburn 35
Samford 7

Samford	0	7	0	0 —7
Auburn	14	14	7	0 —35

First Quarter
Aub—Sanders 18 pass from White (Etheridge kick)
Aub—Bailey 50 pass from White (Etheridge kick)
Second Quarter
Aub—Davis 1 run (Etheridge kick)
Sam—Green 24 pass from Yancey (Ingram kick)
Aub—Sanders 53 pass from White (Etheridge kick)
Third Quarter
Aub—Davis 10 run (Etheridge kick)
Attendance— 68,936.

	Sam	Aub
First downs	16	18
Rushes-yards	34-140	45-180
Passing	120	229
Return Yards	22	75
Comp-Att-Int	13-31-2	10-15-0
Punts	8-35	6-47
Fumbles-Lost	2-1	0-0
Penalties-Yards	7-40	7-39
Time of Possession	30:00	30:00

INDIVIDUALS
SAMFORD
Rushing
Player	Att.	Yds.	TD	Long
Yancey	1	-11	0	0
Ellis	13	46	0	13
Magee	4	38	0	17
Hines	9	52	0	20
Jordan	5	5	0	5
Porter	2	10	0	16

Passing
Player	A-C-I	Yds	TD	Long
Yancey	30-13-1	120	1	24
Jordan	1-0-1	0	0	0

Receiving
Player	No.	Yds	TD	Long
Green	5	52	1	24
Magee	3	34	0	13
NcFadden	1	13	0	13
Hines	1	-2	0	0
Smith	1	15	0	15
Marshall	1	3	0	3

Punting
Player	No.	Yds	Avg	Long
Holmes	8	283	35.3	41

Returns
Player	Punts	Kickoff	Int.
Durgin		3-99	
Porter	2-22		

AUBURN
Rushing
Player	Att.	Yds.	TD	Long
White	6	-27	0	7
Bostic	10	48	0	10
Richardson	2	7	0	4
Davis	18	122	2	48
Nix	1	16	0	0
Frazier	2	8	0	6
Bryan	3	5	0	5
Malcom	2	24	0	22
Sullivan	1	9	0	9

Passing
Player	A-C-I	Yds	TD	Long
White	14-9-0	197	3	53
Nix	1-1-0	32	0	32

Receiving
Player	No.	Yds	TD	Long
Morrow	1	0	0	0
Dom	2	39	0	23
Sanders	2	71	2	53
Bailey	2	59	1	50
McCorvey	1	9	0	9
Fuller	1	19	0	19
Goodson	1	32	0	32

Punting
Player	No.	Yds	Avg	Long
Daniel	6	281	46.8	51

Returns
Player	Punts	Kickoff	Int.
Bailey	1-0	2-40	
Harris			1-4
Robinson			1-26
Carder	2-37		
Battle	2-8		

DEFENSE
SAMFORD
Tackles, assists — O'Neal 3-1; Roberts 1-1; Morris 1-0; Durgin 1-0; Johnson 7-0; Brown 4-1; Craig 2-0; Golden 3-3; Emerson 3-6; Perkins 2-0; Reynolds 1-0; Mobley 3-1; Mansell 1-0; Packer 7-3; Love 2-0; Harris 1-0; James 4-3; Hooks 1-0; Vernon 1-4; Dale 2-0; Peterson 1-0; Battles 1-0; Noblitt 1-0; Holmes 1-0; Goss 1-0; Mangus 1-0.

Sacks — Packer 1, Mobley 2, O'Neal 1. **Fumbles recovered** — None. **Passes intercepted** — None.
AUBURN
Tackles, assists — Mounds 2-1; Shelling 5-2; Johnson 6-2; Pina 0-1; NcGee 3-0; Solomon 3-1; Miska 3-4; Mostella 2-1; Pelton 1-0; Harris 5-3; Thornton 1-2; Robinson 1-1; Primus 2-1; Whitehead 5-2; Luster 1-2; Miller 0-2; Walker 4-2; Hart 1-0; Karoska 1-0; Bryan 2-0; Etheridge 1-0; Milford 0-1; Walker 1-0.

Sacks — Walker 1. **Fumbles recovered** — Shelling, Bryan. **Passes intercepted** — Harris, Robinson. **Passes broken up** — Harris.

AUBURN SEASON
Results (2-0)

Sept. 2	Ole Miss, Won 16-14
Sept. 11	Samford, Won 35-7
Sept. 18	at LSU
Sept. 25	Southern Miss
Oct. 2	at Vandy
Oct. 9	Miss. State
Oct. 16	Florida
Oct. 30	at Arkansas
Nov. 6	New Mexico St.
Nov. 13	at Georgia
Nov. 20	Alabama

Strong safety Brian Robinson (20) and defensive tackle Damon Primus (77) celebrate a take-away against LSU. It was a big night for Auburn on both sides of the ball.
Steve Barnett photo

AN OFFENSIVE SHOW
Louisiana State

Bowden's Tigers slam LSU 34-10

Neal Sims, News staff writer

BATON ROUGE, La.—LSU was primed for a party once Auburn was run out of town.

Auburn hit the road all right, but when the visiting Tigers left town, they had a new all-time pass-ing leader and an old image revived.

Auburn dismantled LSU 34-10 Saturday night, scoring three touchdowns in the second quarter, then putting the game away with a strong second half. Along the way, quarterback Stan White became Auburn's passing yardage leader with one of the best performances of his career, and the tail-back duo of James Bostic and Stephen Davis combined for 205 yards rushing.

The victory, before a crowd of 71,936 in Tiger Stadium, put an end to a discouraging streak on

Coach Bowden sends his offense onto the field, where they stayed and enjoyed success much of the night.
Steve Barnette photo

Auburn's defense got in its licks, too. Here defensive end Andre Miller closes in just as the LSU quarterback releases the ball.

Steve Barnette photo

the road for Auburn, a team that had won only one Southeastern Conference game away from home in the past two seasons.

Unbeaten Auburn (3-0 overall, 2-0 in the SEC) continued its string of early success under new coach Terry Bowden. Rebuilding LSU (1-2, 1-1) was foiled in its effort to get off to a winning start at home. "This is obviously a great win for Auburn," said Bowden. "There were some concerns about playing on the road. We made a lot of mistakes because of the crowd noise. This is a tough place to play, and that's what makes this win so important."

White, who threw for 282 yards and completed 20 of his 28 passes, said, "I'm totally excited about breaking the record, but it's a one-night celebration."

LSU coach Curley Hallman said, "I don't have to look at the films to see the difference in the ballgame. It's taking that piece of leather and doing some things with it."

LSU did get going early when freshman Eddie "Boo" Kennison, who had gained 202 all-purpose yards against Mississippi State the week before, broke a punt return for 55 yards to set up LSU at the Auburn 35.

The touchdown came on a 10-yard pass from quarterback Jamie Howard to flanker Scott Ray and gave LSU a 7-0 lead with just over four minutes played.

The LSU defense stopped Auburn again in three plays, but this time Auburn punter Terry Daniel never game Kennison a chance, punting a 63-yarder out of bounds at the LSU 5.

On the first play from there, AU defensive end Gary Walker broke through and nailed LSU tailback Germaine Williams, bringing him down in the end zone. An official, however, ruled Williams down by contact at the goal line and took the safety off the scoreboard.

Auburn came roaring back in the second quarter, putting three touchdowns on the scoreboard with a number of big plays.

First, White connected for 39 yards to wideout

Frank Sanders, a play that made White Auburn's all-time career passing yardage leader. After a 31-yard run by Bostic got to the LSU 1, White sneaked in for the touchdown.

Auburn got field position when LSU's Howard, scrambling for 11 yards, fumbled and Jason Miska recovered for Auburn at the LSU 30. Auburn scored in two plays. Fullback Tony Richardson was wide open over the middle, and White hit him at the 13. Then Bostic bounced outside and went around left end for the touchdown.

Auburn made it 21-7, covering 85 yards in three plays. The drive got moving on a 25-yard pass from White to Sanders. Then, on a fake reverse to Sanders, wideout Thomas Bailey ran free behind everybody, and White laid in the pass for a 57-yard score.

In the third quarter, Auburn marched 86 yards in 14 plays to score again. Passes to running backs Harold Morrow and Reid McMilion got Auburn past midfield. White tried two deep passes to Sanders, one barely too long and the other broken up in the end zone.

After Auburn got a first down inside the 24, tight end Derrick Dorn took a pass to the 1, and White sneaked in for his second rushing touchdown to put Auburn ahead 28-7.

Then LSU got a big play, a 53-yard run by fullback Jermaine Sharp to the Auburn 5. Three plays later, LSU was no closer, and Andre Lafleur's 22-yard field goal made it 28-10.

A 19-yard run by Bostic and a 9-yard scramble by White, plus a 15-yard penalty for a late hit on the quarterback, put Auburn at the LSU 27. Auburn closed the drive, eventually settling for a 24-yard field goal by Scott Etheridge on the first play of the fourth quarter to make it 31-10.

An interception by Otis Mounds set up Auburn's last score. Etheridge, still perfect on the year, hit a 36-yard field goal for the 34-10 final.

Auburn cracks poll at no. 25

Neal Sims News staff writer

AUBURN—It's Jamie Howard talking, and can you believe this?

He's the LSU quarterback, and his team had just been throttled 34-10 by Auburn.

"I'm really confused right now," said Howard. "We were the better team. We had more talent."

Said Auburn coach Terry Bowden, when told Sunday of Howard's remarks, "Excuse me." Bowden's Tigers dominated Howard's Tigers, rolling up 554 yards on offense and defensively holding Howard to just nine completions in 36 passes for 103 yards.

Generously, Bowden added, "Jamie is a fine quarterback. I think he has as much or more talent as anybody on our football team. Scores are always the final indicator."

The victory put unbeaten Auburn (3-0 overall, 2-0 in the Southeastern Conference) back in the national rankings for the first time in nearly two years. The Tigers, lurking around the top 25 the past two weeks, are No. 25 this week in the Associated Press poll.

Auburn 34, LSU 10

THE YARDSTICK

Auburn	0	21	7	6—	34
LSU	7	0	3	0—	10

First Quarter
LSU—Ray 10 pass from Howard (Lafleur kick)

Second Quarter
AUB—White 1 run (Etheridge kick)
AUB—Bostic 13 run (Etheridge kick)
AUB—Bailey 57 pass from White (Etheridge kick)

Third Quarter
AUB—White 1 run (Etheridge kick)
LSU—FG Lafleur 22

Fourth Quarter
AUB—FG Etheridge 24
AUB—FG Etheridge 36
Attendance— 71,936

	Aub	LSU
First downs	27	11
Rushes-yards	48-281	26-157
Passing	289	103
Return Yards	38	79
Comp-Att-Int	21-30-0	9-37-1
Punts	5-244	10-395
Fumbles-Lost	4-3	3-1
Penalties-Yards	13-110	6-78
Time of Possession	37:27	22:33

INDIVIDUALS

AUBURN

Rushing

Player	Att.	Yds.	TD	Long
Bostic	13	110	1	31
Davis	16	95	0	38
White	10	17	2	16
Frazier	2	13	0	11
Richardson	4	10	0	3
Sanders	1	10	0	10
Bryan	1	7	0	7
Malcom	1	3	0	3

Passing

Player	A-C-I	Yds	TD	Long
White	28-20-0	282	1	57
Nix	2-1-0	7	0	7

Receiving

Player	No.	Yds	TD	Long
Richardson	6	59	0	17
Sanders	6	95	0	38
McMilion	3	20	0	14
Dorn	2	21	0	19
Bailey	2	67	1	57
Gosha	1	7	0	7
Morrow	1	20	0	20

Punting

Player	No.	Yds	Avg	Long
Daniel	5	244	48.8	63

Returns

Player	Punts	Kickoff	Int.

| Bailey | 4-14 | 3-57 | |
| Battle | 1-9 | | |

LSU

Rushing

Player	Att.	Yds.	TD	Long
Sharp	5	53	0	53
Johnson	7	28	0	15
Howard	2	26	0	15
Davis	5	24	0	9
Butler	1	6	0	6
Williams	4	6	0	7
Toomer	1	0	0	0
Holstein	1	1	0	1

Passing

Player	A-C-I	Yds	TD	Long
Howard	36-9-1	103	1	22
Loup	1-0-0	0	0	0

Receiving

Player	No.	Yds	TD	Long
Bech	4	53	0	22
Ray	1	10	0	10
Johnson	1	6	0	6
Bishop	1	17	0	17
Wilson	1	5	0	5
Kennison	1	12	0	12

Punting

Player	No.	Yds	Avg	Long
Holstein	10	395	39.5	52

Returns

Player	Punts	Kickoff	Int.
Kennison	3-79	4-95	

DEFENSE

AUBURN

Tackles, assists —G.Walker 7-0; Shelling 6-0; Solomon 3-1; Miller 3-0; Mounds 3-0; Miska 2-0; Harris 1-1; Mostella 1-0; Daniel 1-0; Primus 1-0; A.Etheridge 1-0; Crook 1-0; Pina 1-0; Ja.Bryan 1-0.

Sacks - None. Passes Intercepted Mounds 1.

LSU

Tackles, assists —Northern 9-1; Washington 4-5; Deshotel 6-2; Hilliard 5-2; Calais 5-1; Marshall 5-0; Young 4-0; White 3-0; B.Williams 3-0; James 2-1; N.Miller 3-0; Walker 2-0; Huffman 1-1; Pegues 2-0; Hewitt 1-1; Gillyard 2-0; Bellis 0-2; L.Williams 1-0; Toomer 1-0; Setters 1-0; Kessler 1-0; Johnson 1-0; Pullett 1-0; R.Miller 1-0; Thibodeaux 1-0; Crawford 1-0; C.Howard 0-1; Taylor 0-1; C.Burks 1-0; Hankton 0-1; Crowell 0-1.

Sacks - None.

AUBURN SEASON
Results (3-0)

Sept. 2	Ole Miss, Won 16-14
Sept. 11	Samford, Won 35-7
Sept. 18	at LSU, Won 34-10
Sept. 25	Southern Miss
Oct. 2	at Vandy
Oct. 9	Miss. State
Oct. 16	Florida
Oct. 30	at Arkansas
Nov. 6	New Mexico St.
Nov. 13	at Georgia
Nov. 20	Alabama

"I don't have to look at the films to see the difference in the ballgame.

LSU Coach Curly Hallman

Stan White rears back for a pass against USM. He and the offense generated enough points to overcome an error-prone performance.
Steve Barnette photo

WINNING UGLY
Southern Mississippi

Auburn overcomes miscues, whips USM

Neal Sims, News staff writer

AUBURN—Six fumbles can be dreadfully dis-turbing. Five touchdowns can be even more comforting.

That was the bottom line for unbeaten Auburn Saturday as the Tigers did away with old nemesis Southern Mississippi, winning 35-24 in a game that at times got a bit shoddy.

"That was a great win for us because we did so many things to lose, and we won the football game," said Auburn coach Terry Bowden. "There was a time when we did those things and lost."

Terry Bowden strikes a pose more like a mistro than a football coach during the game against Southern Mississippi. The offense hit a few sour notes, but still won the day.
Steve Barnette photo

Auburn 35
Southern Miss 24

So.Miss	7	0	17	0—	24
Auburn	14	7	7	7—	35

First Quarter
USM—Brock 47 pass from Bentley (Lomoro kick)
Aub—Bostic 3 run (Etheridge kick)
Aub—Bostic 4 run (Etheridge kick)
Second Quarter
Aub—Davis 2 run (Etheridge kick)
Third Quarter
USM—Owens 39 pass from Bentley (Lomoro kick)
USM—FG Lomoro 20
USM—Jackson 11 interception return (Lomoro kick)
Aub—Bailey 40 pass from White (Etheridge kick)
Fourth Quarter
Aub—Bostic 6 run (Etheridge kick)
Attendance—83,476

	USM	Aub
First downs	9	21
Rushes-yards	30-145	55-261
Passing	158	158
Return Yards	54	64
Comp-Att-Int	8-23-1	12-22-1
Punts	8-47	6-51
Fumbles-Lost	2-2	6-2
Penalties-Yards	3-35	4-52
Time of Possession	23:05	36:55

INDIVIDUALS
SOUTHERN MISS
Rushing

Player	Att.	Yds.	TD	Long
Bentley	2	8	0	2
Jones	6	20	0	9
Boyd	17	90	0	47
McGee	4	36	0	27
McKinney	1	7	0	7

Passing

Player	A-C-I	Yds	TD	Long
Bentley	23-8-1	158	2	47

Receiving

Player	No.	Yds	TD	Long
Pearson	1	6	0	6
Brock	3	64	1	47
Owens	2	50	1	39
Boyd	1	34	0	34
Montgomery	1	4	0	4

Punting

Player	No.	Yds	Avg	Long
Estes	8	376	47	61

Returns

Player	Punts	Kickoff	Int.
Gulley	2-30	1-17	
Carter	2-13		
Thomas		1-16	
Gamble			1-9
Boyd		1-29	
Jackson			1-11

AUBURN
Rushing

Player	Att.	Yds.	TD	Long
White	6	-14	0	2
Bostic	25	116	3	16
Richardson	5	14	0	6
Davis	14	66	1	18
McMilion	6	76	0	64

Passing

Player	A-C-I	Yds	TD	Long
White	22-12-1	158	1	40

Receiving

Player	No.	Yds	TD	Long
Sanders	5	79	0	30
Bailey	3	56	1	10
Richardson	1	1	0	1
McMilion	1	15	0	15
Morrow	1	2	0	2
Dorn	1	7	0	7

Punting

Player	No.	Yds	Avg	Long
Daniel	6	307	51.2	62

Returns

Player	Punts	Kickoff	Int.
Bailey	4-56	1-13	
Robinson			1-8

DEFENSE
SOUTHERN MISS
Tackles, assists —Rankins 5-0; Wright 0-1; Gamble 3-0; Harvey 2-1; 4-1; Harmon 1-2; Gulley 5-3; Ratcliff 6-0; McRae 4-1; Harris 0-1; Nix 5-0; Adams 3-1; Walthaw 5-0; Carter 0-1; Jackson 2-1; Tobias 2-0; Hamilton 3-0; Elder 0-2; Johnson 1-0; Smith 1-0; Stabler 1-0; Crawford 1-0; Watterson 2-2; Beckwith 2-2; Nunn 2-0; Thomas 1-0.
Sacks —Beckwith 1. Fumbles recovered — Adams, Walthaw, Gamble. Passes intercepted — Jackson. Passes broken up — Carter, Nunn.

AUBURN
Tackles, assists — Mounds 1-2; Shelling 8-0; Jackson 3-0; Johnson 0-1; Robinson 2; Solomon 5-2; Miska 6-5; Mostella 1-2; Pe 2-1; Harris 1-5; Thornton 1-1; Primus 1-3; Whitehead 3-1; Miller 0-1; Walker 1-0; Hart 2-2; Morrow 2-0; Malcom 0-1; Etheridge 1-0; Riggins 0-1; Gandy 1-0.
Sacks —None. Fumbles recovered — Harris, Davis, White, Mostella, Bostic. Passes intercepted — Robinson. Passes broken up — Jackson 2, Mostella, Harris.

AUBURN SEASON
Results (4-0)

Sept. 2	Ole Miss, Won	16-12
Sept. 11	Samford, Won	35-7
Sept. 18	at LSU, Won	34-10
Sept. 25	Southern Miss, Won	35-24
Oct. 2	at Vandy	
Oct. 9	Miss. State	
Oct. 16	Florida	
Oct. 30	at Arkansas	
Nov. 6	New Mexico St.	
Nov. 13	at Georgia	
Nov. 20	Alabama	

touchdown, and took the lead 24-21 before the Tigers closed out the game with two more TDs.

"I'm excited about this win, and I won't let those things detract," said Bowden. "We won't take it as a step backward. We'll take 4-0. As much as we're going to have to talk about the poor execution, I'm not going to lose any sleep until tomorrow."

Southern Miss also lost two fumbles, both coming on dropped punts, and Golden Eagles coach Jeff Bower lamented, "There were a lot of crucial mistakes. It was a real sloppy game on both sides."

Bowden said Southern Miss works hard at stealing the football, and it paid off some Saturday in front of a crowd of 83,476 at Jordan-Hare Stadium.

"Southern Miss is the best tackling team, as far as stripping the football, that I've ever seen," he said. "We knew coming in that they practice it. We'll take the blame, and should, but I give a lot of the credit to them."

Auburn tailback James Bostic, in fact, fumbled the first two times he touched the ball and had several other bobbles. He recovered, though, to rush for 116 yards and three of the Tigers' touchdowns. "I think you've got to separate effort from execution," said Bowden. "These boys never got down when they got behind. The execution was not good, and the coaches have to take responsibility for that.

"We got behind in the third quarter, and momentum was completely the other way. Our men came back. The defense got tough, and our offense had some long drives."

Auburn (4-0 overall, 2-0 in the Southeastern Conference) left the football on the ground six times and lost two of the fumbles. Southern Miss (1-2) rallied with 17 points in the third quarter, one score coming on a pass interception returned for a

Of his team's charge from behind, Bower said, "We felt like if we could come up with a big play or two and get some points on the board, then we could get back in the game. That's exactly what we did. We got ahead. We just couldn't hold on."

Southern Mississippi took the lead early, scoring its first touchdown just three minutes into the game.

Auburn free safety Brian Robinson intercepted a pass on Southern Miss' first possession, setting up Auburn at the USM 46. But Bostic fumbled it right back to the Golden Eagles on Auburn's first offensive snap.

Southern then covered 56 yards in two plays to take a 7-0 lead. First, tailback Barry Boyd gained 9. Then quarterback Kevin Bentley, under pressure and scrambling toward the sideline, found flanker Fred Brock open downfield, connected with him around the Auburn 30, and Brock threaded his way in from there for the score. Bostic dropped the ball again on Auburn's second play from scrimmage, but this time he got it back after losing 5 yards. Then it was Southern's turn for a turnover. Trying to return a 52-yard punt by Terry Daniel, USM's Perry Daniel fumbled, and Anthony Harris recovered for Auburn at the USM 16.

Bostic got the touchdown from the 5 for a 7-7 tie.

"The score picked me back up," said Bostic. "I was down on myself." The Tigers opened their next possession with a 30-yard play. Quarterback Stan White faked to Bostic, then hit wide receiver Frank Sanders at the USM 30. Bostic rambled at right end for 16 yards, then White completed a pass to wideout Thomas Bailey at the 5. Bostic got his second touchdown from 3 yards out to put Auburn up 14-7.

The Auburn defense choked Southern in the second quarter. Another Auburn fumble, this one by Sanders after making a catch, set up the Golden Eagles at their own 45. Three plays gained nothing.

Later in the half, Boyd broke a 47-yard run to the Auburn 19, but on a fourth-and-one try from the 10, Boyd was stacked up for no gain.

Auburn took over, and on its first play, fullback Reid McMillion broke through the middle on a 64-yard run. Southern defensive back Melvin Ratcliff ran him down from behind and stripped the ball, but Auburn's Stephen Davis recovered at the USM 26.

Davis gained 9 up the middle, and Richardson got the first down at the 15. A throw to Sanders gave Auburn a first-and-goal at the 5. Bostic ran twice, then Davis scored the touchdown from 2

yards out, completing the 90-yard drive with less than a minute to play in the half and Auburn ahead 21-7.

Southern Miss came charging back in the third quarter. On a third-and-seven play from the Auburn 39, tight end Anthony Owens, who had played at Auburn High School, ran uncovered around the 25, caught a pass and raced in for the score.

Southern's Carter fumbled another punt later in the quarter at his own 39. But Auburn tailback Harold Morrow gave it right back, fumbling after making a catch.

Bentley threw to Boyd for 34 yards, and fullback Howard McGee got loose for another 27 as the Golden Eagles drove close again. But three plays from the Auburn 7 left Southern short, and kicker Johnny Lomoro of Midfield hit a 20-yard field goal to cut Auburn's lead to 21-17.

On the Tigers' second play, White was under pressure and being chased when he threw, and Southern defensive tackle Kevin Jackson made a clean catch of the pass interception. His 11-yard touchdown return put USM up 24-21.

Just 38 seconds until the end of the quarter, however, White and wideout Bailey teamed up to bring Auburn back."I went to the line," said White, "looked at their deep safety, and he was so far in I thought Thomas could beat him one-on-one. I had a feeling he had him beat."

Said Bailey, "I had to get around the defensive back. I believe if he had turned around, he could have broken up the pass. Stan did a great job of laying it out, and I broke around him to catch the ball."

The result was a 40-yard touchdown play, Bailey beating LaBarion Rankins in the end zone for the catch that put Auburn ahead to stay.

"We never played very well after that play," said USM's Bower.

The Tigers closed it out with an 87-yard drive in the fourth quarter, capped by a 6-yard run by Bostic for the score.

Finding a way to win, Auburn defenders put up a magnificent goal-line stand that preserved victory against Vanderbilt.
Steve Barnette photo

FINDING A WAY TO WIN
Vanderbilt

Unbeaten Auburn puts squeeze on Vanderbilt

Neal Sims, News staff writer

NASHVILLE, Tenn.—Here in Music City, as a current clever country line goes, "Sometimes you're the windshield; sometimes you're the bug."

Vanderbilt football, though, is most always the bug and was once again Saturday night.

Unbeaten and at times uninspired Auburn did the driving this time, wiping off Vanderbilt 14-10 despite a flimsy first half. The Tigers needed two long second-half drives on offense, one for the winning touchdown and another to eat the clock, and a stunning goal-line stand by the defense to keep their remarkable season perfect.

To Auburn coach Terry Bowden, the strong finish meant more than the struggling start. "That was clearly the best win we've had all year," he said. "I saw a team that would not lose a football game. They were going to find a way to win, and that's one thing we've been looking for at Auburn for a long time."

Auburn (5-0 overall, 3-0 in the Southeastern Conference) continued its best start in seven seasons under their new coach. For Vanderbilt (1-3, 0-3), it was another faulty start to a season and another tough setback for coach Gerry DiNardo, in his third year of trying to build a Vandy program.

The Tigers, going in as the No. 23 team in the country, won their third consecutive SEC victory, their second on the road this year, and their eighth straight against the Commodores.

The Auburn offense couldn't get going early before the Vanderbilt Stadium crowd of 40,527. The Tigers' woeful first-half showing included no points and just 11 yards rushing. It was the Auburn defense that put up the first points and saved the game at the end, stopping the Commodores four times at the Tigers' goal line.

"I told our team," said DiNardo, "we played physical and with a lot of emotion, but you have to score when you get down on the goal line."

Said Bowden, "I've got to give a lot of credit to Vanderbilt. I'm not going to say they deserved to lose the football game. We got a few more points in the end, and when we had to stop them on fourth-and-goal that was a big play."

Vanderbilt ground out one long touchdown drive and burned Auburn with a long punt return to set up another score and take a halftime lead.

Auburn's offense got the ball only once in the opening quarter and came out throwing. Quarterback Stan White completed five of his first seven passes before the drive ended at the Vandy 26 on a botched snap in the shotgun formation.

Kicker Scott Etheridge's 43-yard field-goal attempt drifted wide right, his first miss of the season, and Auburn came up empty.

Then the Tigers' defense struck for the game's first score. Vandy had picked up a first down on the ground, mostly on fullback dives, when quarterback Kenny Simon tried to throw to his fullback. Auburn free safety Brian Robinson stepped in front of Royce Love, picked off the throw and ran it back 45 yards for the touchdown and a 7-0 Auburn lead.

Vandy never went to the pass on its next drive, and the Commodores ground attack chewed out a 72-yard march in 11 plays to tie the game.

The 'Dores moved the ball past midfield in

the second quarter, breaking a seven-quarter string of playing offense at their own end of the field. Tailback Tony Jackson broke big runs of 14 and 21 yards to take Vandy to the Auburn 3. Three plays later, Love got the touchdown from the 1.

The long punt return set up Vandy's next score as the Commodores grabbed the lead right before halftime. Jeff Brothers made the play, breaking through the Auburn coverage and running back the punt 39 yards to set up Vandy at the Auburn 32.

Vandy got no closer, however, and kicker Steve Yenner had to get the three points twice. First, Yenner hit a 49-yard field goal, but that was wiped out by a formation penalty against Vanderbilt for not enough men on the line of scrimmage. So Yenner then hit a 53-yard field goal, the third longest in Vandy history and the longest of his career, to put Vandy ahead 10-7 with seven seconds left in the first half.

The Tigers' offense, which had gained only 64 yards in the first half, began to click in the third quarter as Auburn controlled the ball for nine plays on a 83-yard touchdown drive. The big play was a 52-yard throw from White to wide receiver Frank Sanders that took the Tigers to the Vandy 4. Two blasts by tailback James Bostic scored the TD and put the Tigers out front again 14-10.

Steady Vandy came right back, again pounding the Auburn defense with its running attack, but when the Commodores got close the Tigers closed them down with the goal-line stand.

Vandy began the drive at its 29 and reeled off three quick first downs. Then Simon kept the ball on a quarterback option for a 25-yard gain, and two pitches to tailback Jermaine Johnson got the Commodores their fifth first down of the drive at the Auburn 3 on the final play of the third quarter.

That set up the defensive stand. Three times, the Tigers stuffed different Vandy run-

Auburn tacklers Mike Pelton (50), Derrick Robinson (58), Otis Mounds (2) and Anthony Harris (53) made life miserable for Vandy's offense much of the game.
Steve Barnette photo

ners. On fourth down from the 1, linebacker Anthony Harris caught Johnson in his dive in mid-air and hurled him back.

"It was a complete defensive effort," said Harris. "I just hit the guy when he tried to dive over."

The Tigers' offense controlled the ball most of the rest of the way. One 15-play drive was stopped at the Vandy 2, and the Tigers killed the clock on their last possession at the Vandy 1.

Auburn 14
Vanderbilt 10

Auburn	7	0	7	0—14
Vanderbilt	0	10	0	0—10

First Quarter
Aub—Robinson 45 int. return (Etheridge kick)
Second Quarter
Aub—Van—Love 1 run (Yenner kick)
Van—FG Yenner 53
Third Quarter
Aub—Bostic 2 run (Etheridge kick)
Attendance— 40,527

	Aub	Van
First downs	18	13
Rushes-yards	36-85	53-217
Passing	145	7
Return Yards	53	43
Comp-Att-Int	12-20-0	1-4-1
Punts	4-40	4-38
Fumbles-Lost	2-0	2-1
Penalties-Yards	5-37	8-85
Time of Possession	27:16	32:44

INDIVIDUALS
AUBURN
Rushing

Player	Att.	Yds.	TD	Long
White	11	-15	0	3
Bostic	16	55	1	14
Richardson	3	11	0	0
McMillon	2	6	0	4
Davis	4	28	0	14

Passing

Player	A-C-I	Yds	TD	Long
White	20-12-0	145	0	52

Receiving

Player	No.	Yds	TD	Long
Bostic	1	0	0	0
Richardson	4	30	0	12
Sanders	5	94	0	52
Fuller	1	7	0	7
Carder	1	14	0	14

Punting

Player	No.	Yds	Avg	Long
Daniel	4	161	40.3	59

Returns

Player	Punts	Kickoff	Int.
Bailey	2-8	1-25	
McCovery		1-8	

VANDERBILT
Rushing

Player	Att.	Yds.	TD	Long
Johnson	8	32	0	9
Simon	12	55	0	25
Douglas	1	-4	0	-4
Halmers	3	21	0	13
Lewis	2	-3	0	0
Jackson	13	67	0	21
Love	14	49	1	9

Passing

Player	A-C-I	Yds	TD	Long
Simon	2-1-1	7	0	7

Receiving

Player	No.	Yds	TD	Long
Ware	1	7	0	7

Punting

Player	No.	Yds	Avg	Long
Darringl	4	152	38	44

Returns

Player	Punts	Kickoff	Int.
Brothers	2-43		
Jackson	2-54		

DEFENSE
AUBURN
Tackles, assists —Harris 4-9; Whitehead 0-1; Miller 1-0; Primus 3-2; Hart 7-0; Pelton 2-2; Walker 2-0; Etheridge 0-1; Solomon 3-1; Mostella 2-2; Jackson 3-0; Mounds 2-0; Miska 6-5; D Robinson 5-2; B Robinson 8-2; Johnson 2-0; Shelling 6-1; Rina 1-0; Daniel 1-0. Sacks —None.Fumbles recovered —Whitehead 1. Passes intercepted —B Robinson 1. Passes broken up —None.
VANDERBILT
Tackles, assists —Quarles 4-3; DeWitt 3-0; Boykin 2-1; Manley 8-2; Sullivan 1-1; Young 5-0; Francis 6-2; King 2-3; Finklin 0-1; Smith 3-1; Collins 4-5; Brothers 5-2; Davis 4-1. Sacks —Manley 2. Fumbles recovered —None. Passes intercepted —None. Passes broken up —Boykin 1; Brothers 1; Davis 1.

AUBURN SEASON
Results (5-0)

Sept. 2	Ole Miss, Won 16-12
Sept. 11	Samford, Won 35-7
Sept. 18	at LSU, Won 34-10
Sept. 25	Southern Miss, Won 35-24
Oct. 2	at Vandy, Won 14-10
Oct. 9	Miss. State
Oct. 16	Florida
Oct. 30	at Arkansas
Nov. 6	New Mexico St.
Nov. 13	at Georgia
Nov. 20	Alabama

Auburn has Hart in goal-line stand

Jay Waid, Special to The News

NASHVILLE, Tenn.—Auburn defender Randy Hart nearly went crazy, jumping up and down when it became apparent Vandy was going for it on fourth-and-goal at the Auburn 1 early in the fourth quarter.

He welcomed the challenge. He said he knew Vandy wasn't getting in the end zone to retake the lead on the Tigers.

Linebacker Anthony Harris made Hart look like a prophet when he stuck Jermaine Johnson short of the goal.

Harris called it the best lick of his Auburn career.

Terry Bowden called it the pivotal play in the game which preserved the 14-10 win in Vanderbilt Stadium.

"We weren't gonna let 'em in," Hart said. "I told the guys that Vandy was not coming in. I said, 'We're gonna hold 'em.'

"And we did, and it took all the confidence away from Vandy. This is the way we're gonna play from now on."

Said Harris, "It was a do-or-die situation. It was the best hit I've put on anybody since I've been at Auburn.

"And it's more special since it came on a play that meant so much."

Harris called the goal-line stand a "complete defensive effort and agreed that Hart had much to do with the fourth-down play. "He's a leader," Harris said. "He said we couldn't give them anything. We couldn't even let them lean our way."

"It was a magnificent defensive stand," Bowden said. "The defense went and did it. And that play by Anthony Harris was the big turning point in the game.

"That was clearly the best win we've had all year. I saw more character out there. . .I saw a team that would not lose a football game. They found a way to win.

"And you have to give a lot of credit to Vandy. They came after us in every way they could. I thought they had a great football team." Because of Vandy's ball-control I-Bone, Auburn never got untracked offensively, but it did come up with one big passing play—a 52-yarder from Stan White to Frank Sanders _ to set up James Bostic's third-quarter TD that turned out to be the game's last points. "Our offense wasn't on the field very much," Sanders said, "but we got one when we needed it. It didn't matter if it was me or Thomas Bailey who caught it.

"But we still haven't put it all together. You haven't seen the total package yet."

Said White, "We hardly ever had the ball. We just had to exploit their secondary when we could."

The other AU touchdown was a 45-yard interception return by Brian Robinson. "I was just reading the flow of the play." said Robinson. "I saw the fullback in the flat. I was expecting the option and the flow took me to the fullback. The quarterback (Kenny Simon) threw it and I broke on it. It was wide open to the end zone from there."

Did Bowden dream he would start 5-0? "I dreamed it. It starts there. I couldn't be happier," he said.

"All the credit goes to the players. They're the ones who made the commitment. An advancement is ahead of us. We've won as many games right now as Auburn won in the past two years."

"I saw a team that would not lose a football game. They were going to find a way to win, and that's one thing we've been looking for at Auburn for a long time."
—Coach Terry Bowden

Mississippi State University ball carrier tries vainly to push away an Auburn defender, but the swarming defense held the Bulldogs in check.

Mark Almond photo

WHIPPING ADVERSITY
Mississippi State

6-0 Unbeaten Tigers roll past State

Neal Sims, News staff writer

AUBURN—The Auburn offense giveth. The Auburn defense taketh away.

What the offense gave away was the football—four turnovers in the first 20 minutes of play against Mississippi State Saturday. What the defense took away was the scoring chances—holding the Bulldogs to just two field goal despite all the early gifts.

The result, once the Tigers hardy running game and big-play passing offense got rolling, was a 31-17 victory that sent Auburn unbeaten past the midway point of coach Terry Bowden's first season as head coach.

"I wouldn't say it before," said Bowden, "but I wanted this win very badly. I did not want to come to the Mississippi State game, go out with a loss and have to face what we've got to face."

Auburn (6-0 overall, 4-0 in the Southeastern Conference) answered State's early field goals with three second-quarter touchdowns, then cruised home with ball-control before a Jordan-Hare Stadium crowd of 84,222. Mississippi State (1-4, 0-3) simply left too many men on base as the Bulldogs couldn't cash in on their scoring opportunities.

"It was amazing how everything went wrong to begin with," said Bowden after his team came back after turning over the football to State four times in its first five possessions.

"We just had some fluke interceptions and some strange fumbles," he said. "None of them were enough to stop this football team. Nobody got down, and nobody gave up.

"Everytime we touched the ball, something went wrong. The defense was the key. When things went wrong, they held them to no touchdowns."

State's strategy was to open with a no-huddle offense and throw from the shotgun, trying to disrupt the Auburn defense. It didn't work. Quarterback Todd Jordan, who threw for 405 yards against Florida the week before, got only 155 against the Tigers.

Meanwhile, the Tigers couldn't hold onto the football. State's first punt, booted short, hit Auburn's Chris Shelling in the leg as he was trying to block. The Bulldogs recovered at the Auburn 41, got no closer than the 29 and had to take Tom Burke's 41-yard field goal for a 3-0 lead.

A tipped pass led to the next Auburn turnover, an interception at midfield. This time, Shelling got the ball right back for the Tigers, intercepting Jordan at the Auburn 1.

The Tigers had to punt it out, and State got close enough for Burke to kick a 45-yard field goal to make it 6-0.

Auburn lost the ball a third time in the first quarter on a fumble by James Bostic at its 45. This time, the Tiger defense held State to 2 yards in three plays and forced a punt. A fourth turnover came on a flea-flicker pass attempt by Auburn that was picked off in the State end zone.

"We didn't make the plays," said Mississippi State coach Jackie Sherrill. "We had enough opportunities. When you get six points when you should at least have 14, that's kind of discouraging. It wasn't anything they did at the first, it was what we didn't do."

Then came a penalty on State that turned the game for Auburn. The Bulldogs were flagged for roughing the kicker on a punt, giving the Tigers new life, and Auburn overcame all its offensive misfortune with one big play.

"I don't think they expected us to throw four receivers at them," said quarterback Stan

White, who lined up the Tigers in a spread formation, with three wideouts and a tight end going out.

Wide receiver Frank Sanders got by the strong safety, streaked down the sideline and, said White, "I just had to hit him. Frank did the rest."

Sanders, who caught the 57-yard touchdown pass in stride, said, "We tried to spread the defense out and take away their run support. But this team was so scared of our running, they stayed in that defense. The play went just how they draw it up."

Sanders had been caught from behind last week after a catch at Vanderbilt, but not this time. "They've picked at me all week about that," he said. "I wasn't going to get run down this time."

The Tigers went up 14-6 with an 80-yard drive, keyed by big runs from Bostic, who finished the day with 140 yards rushing. Bostic had gains of 16 and 14 yards to set up the score, a faked draw and a 35-yard screen pass to fellow tailback Stephen Davis.

"It was a screen to the wide side of the field," said White. "The linemen cleaned out the linebackers and the defensive backs. Steve slipped through and broke a tackle and went on in for the touchdown."

Davis, who also had a 100-yard day (70 running, 43 receiving) outraced State defenders for the score. "Once I saw the blockers out there, I knew it was a touchdown. I knew it when I touched it."

An interception by Shelling set up Auburn's third touchdown, a 28-yard drive with the score coming on a 7-yard pass from White to fullback Tony Richardson.

Auburn receiver Frank Sanders breaks free for a gain against MSU defenders.
Steve Barnette photo

Auburn 31
Miss. State 17

Miss. State	6	0	3	8 — 17
Auburn	0	21	7	3 — 31

First Quarter
MSU—FG Burke 41.
MSU—FG Burke 45.
Second Quarter
Aub—Sanders 57 pass from White (Etheridge kick).
Aub—Davis 35 pass from White (Etheridge kick).
Aub—Richardson 7 pass from White (Etheridge kick).
Third Quarter
MSU—FG Burke 31.
Aub—Richardson 3 run (Etheridge kick).
Fourth Quarter
MSU—McCrary 4 pass from Jordan (Jones pass from Jordan).
Aub—FG Etheridge 32.
Attendance— 84,222

	MSU	Aub
First downs	17	24
Rushes-yards	32-130	50-278
Passing	155	186
Return Yards	45	17
Comp-Att-Int	17-41-2	14-24-3
Punts	5-42	2-57
Fumbles-Lost	1-1	2-2
Penalties-Yards	3-25	3-6
Time of Possession	27:23	32:37

INDIVIDUALS
MISSISSIPPI ST.
Rushing

Player	Att.	Yds.	TD	Long
Jordan	3	13	0	10
Davis	13	63	0	14
Bouie	14	43	0	15
Taite	2	11	0	9

Passing

Player	A-C-I	Yds	TD	Long
Jordan	39-17-2	155	1	18
Bouie	1-0-0	0	0	0
Taite	1-0-0	0	0	0

Receiving

Player	No.	Yds	TD	Long
Clark	4	46	0	16
Euell	2	27	0	18
Bouie	3	31	0	18
Davis	2	-2	0	2
McCrary	3	-3	1	7
Moulds	2	34	0	18
Jones	1	16	0	16

Punting

Player	No.	Yds	Avg	Long
Jordan	5	209	41.8	52

Returns

Player	Punts	Kickoff	Int.
Bouie		1-14	
Euell	1-14		
Leasy			1-8
Harris			1-20
Long			1-3

AUBURN
Rushing

Player	Att.	Yds.	TD	Long
White	6	14	0	20
Bostic	10	140	0	19
Richardson	5	25	1	9
Davis	13	70	0	22
McMilion	5	20	0	6
Sanders	1	9	0	9

Passing

Player	A-C-I	Yds	TD	Long
White	24-14-3	186	3	57

Receiving

Player	No.	Yds	TD	Long
Sanders	3	78	1	57
Bailey	2	20	0	11
Carder	1	9	0	9
Davis	2	43	1	35
McMilion	1	-3	0	-3
Richardson	3	28	1	12
Bostic	2	11	0	11

Punting

Player	No.	Yds	Avg	Long
Daniel	2	113	56.5	67

Returns

Player	Punts	Kickoff	Int.
Bailey	1-9	1-23	
Shelling	1-0		1-0
Jackson			1-8
Davis		1-25	

DEFENSE
MISSISSIPPI ST.
f020 Tackles, assists —Harris 2-0; Luster 3-2; James 3-0; Bennett 4-0; Harris 4-1; Curtis 1-0; Gumina 4-3; Holloway 3-1; Long 8-4; Lindsey 2-2; Curry 4-1; Cagins 3-0; Travis 5-1; Stalworth 1-0; Gibson 1-3; McCullough 1-0; Leasy 3-1; Carroll 6-2; Myles 1-0.

Sacks —Travis. Fumbles recovered —Carroll. Passes Intercepted —Leasy, Harris, Long. Passes broken up — Harris 2.

AUBURN
f020 Tackles, assists —Mounds 7-4; Shelling 4-2; Jackson 2-0; Johnson 1-0; Robinson 5-1; Pina 0-1; Solomon 4-1; Miska 6-6; Mostella 0-3; Pelton 0-2; Harris 4-6; Primus 3-2; Luster 2-1; Miller 0-3; Walker 2-1; Hart 1-2; Etheridge 3-1; Richardson 1-0; Bostic 1-0; Gandy 1-0.

Sacks —None. Fumbles recovered —Walker. Passes Intercepted —Jackson, Shelling. Passes broken up —Jackson 5, Mounds.

AUBURN SEASON
Results (6-0)

Sept. 2	Ole Miss, Won 16-12
Sept. 11	Samford, Won 35-7
Sept. 18	at LSU, Won 34-10
Sept. 25	Southern Miss, Won 35-24
Oct. 2	at Vandy, Won 14-10
Oct. 9	Miss. State, Won 31-17
Oct. 16	Florida
Oct. 30	at Arkansas
Nov. 6	New Mexico St.
Nov. 13	at Georgia
Nov. 20	Alabama

Kicker Scott Etheridge puts up the winning field goal late in the game against Florida.
Hal Yeager photo

A STEP TOWARD GREATNESS
Florida

Super Saturday AU stuns Florida; Tigers win big one

Neal Sims, News staff writer

AUBURN—Son of a gun. Son of the Amazin's.

The head coach is dancing, twirling, sprinting toward midfield. His players are shouting, hugging, running wild. Their fans aren't leaving; they're standing and screaming.

Auburn has roared back and soared past Florida, knocking off the No. 4 team in the nation 38-35 Saturday with a rousing finish as the remarkable Tigers continued their extraordinary run through the 1993 season. Just like the 1972 Tigers, dubbed the Amazin's for being just that, this team touches the incredible. "It

Auburn defenders Gary Walker and Willie Whitehead sandwich Florida's quarterback.
Hal Yeager photo

Tailback James Bostic struts his stuff after a touchdown against the Gators. Tightend Andy Fuller (82) joins in the celebration.
Hal Yeager photo

was exhilarating. I'm ready to tell our fans that you're tied in emotionally now," said Auburn coach Terry Bowden. "You're going with us on the good and the bad. They're hooked into this ride whether they like it or not."

They like it. Bowden and players made a curtain call in front of the fans still celebrating a half-hour after the game was over.

Auburn (7-0 overall, 5-0 in the Southeastern Conference) is the league's only team with a perfect record after knocking off previously unbeaten Florida (5-1, 4-1) before a capacity crowd of 85,214 at Jordan-Hare Stadium.

"I would not have guessed that we could get in a scoring match with Florida and have a chance," said Bowden, whose No. 19 Tigers will rise through the rankings this week. "Needless to say we did, and we won.

"We're good enough to beat a top four team. They can vote us where they want to. I'm not going to say we're a top four team, but this team is good enough to beat a lot of football teams."

The Tigers fell behind the Gators early, yet hung close despite a rough first half. The second-half turnaround saw the Auburn offense rally, scoring 17 points in the fourth quarter. The defense, riddled for 386 yards in the first half, held the explosive Gators to just one more score. The winning score came on a Scott Etheridge field goal with 1;21 to play.

"Today's a BIG day for Auburn," said Bowden. "I always believe we're going to come back and win. Every single time, I honestly believe we're going to win the game.

"I told our players, "Just don't quit trying. Believe me, I've been through this before. Something good is going to happen, and we'll go from there.' "

The Tigers came back to take the lead with second-half scoring drives of 76 and 80 yards, added another touchdown after the second long pass interception of the day, and after Florida came back to tie, won it with a late field goal.

"We had a chance to get a pretty good lead

early, but we made some mistakes," said Florida coach Steve Spurrier. "They outplayed us in the second half, but I'm extremely proud of the way we fought back."

Florida had two scores, a 49-yard field goal and a 60-yard touchdown pass from quarterback Danny Wuerffel to wide receiver Jack Jackson, before Auburn posted a first down.

The Gators were threatening an early blowout, poised at the Auburn 10, when the Tigers defense turned the momentum. Cornerback Calvin Jackson stole a pass and raced 96 yards with Auburn's longest interception in more than 45 years.

"I just stepped in front of the receiver, made the catch and saw green in front of me," said Jackson. "I ran as hard as I could."

Auburn took the lead 14-10 after a 75-yard scoring drive, but Florida scored three times in the final six minutes of the first half to take

charge again.

First, a 38-yard run by Errict Rhett, who rushed for 196 yards, set up Judd Davis' second field goal. Rhett got the next touchdown, run ning untouched for a 24-yard score. And the Gators closed out the half ahead 27-14 as wideout Aubrey Hill got open in a confused Auburn secondary for a 13-yard touchdown pass.

In the second half, the Auburn offense clicked and the defense took control.

"We decided to throw a lot more," said Bowden. "They were going to stop our I-formation run. We said, 'To heck with it.' We put the throwing stuff in. I didn't know how it was going to be, but we aren't too bad at it."

The Tigers opened the second half with a drive to the Gators 18, but Etheridge was wide right on his 35-yard field-goal attempt. Still, said Bowden, "We came back, drove down

Swarmed by Gator defenders, Tiger receiver Frank Sanders knew this game was to be no easy task.
Hal Yeager photo

Mike Pina (23) and Brian Robinson (20) congratulate each other on a fine stop of the Florida quarterback.
Hal Yeager photo

It's time to believe in Bowden

Kevin Scarbinsky, News columnist

I believe. I believe in the father (Bobby Bowden) and the son (Terry Bowden), and I believe that just as the father and his Florida State team banished the unholy ghosts of Miami one week ago, the son and his Auburn team banished the unholy ghosts of probation and degradation on a Saturday afternoon in Jordan-Hare Stadium when the skies parted and the ground shook. I believe the old ghosts vanished Saturday in the mist of a cold rain and the bright lights that glowed through the mist: Auburn 38, Florida 35.

I believe justice comes to everyone, and Auburn 38, Florida 35 was sweet justice for every Auburn player of the last three years who never asked for a handout, every coach who lived by the rules and every fan and booster who realized his greatest contribution to the program was not money but faith.

I believe there are wins that go in the record book and wins that go in the scrapbook, and this stirring affair will be pasted in the memory of every person who was fortunate to serve as witness. I believe there has not been such an outpouring of deep emotion in this house since the cold day Alabama believed would never come, the first day Alabama came to Auburn, and Auburn won the day.

I believe that on some distant day at Florida Field, Bowden and his players may come to regret the day they returned to the

and didn't get anything, but we got it clicking. The defense didn't give up on us. Together we won the football game."

The Tigers ran a reverse with wideout Frank Sanders for 16 yards. Quarterback Stan White scrambled for 11 yards on a third-and-10. A 23-yard pass to fullback Tony Richardson got a touchdown to cut Florida's lead to 27-21.

The Gators drove to the Auburn 27, but two sacks threw Wuerffel back to midfield. Then came Auburn's fourth-quarter rally.

Tailback James Bostic got the first TD on a fourth-down play from the Florida 4. "They had strung the sweep out," he said. "I just turned it back in. I wasn't going to be denied the first down or the touchdown."

field in Jordan-Hare for a victory embrace with their fans. I believe they may regret it, but they will never forget it.

STAN THE MAN

I believe that in 60 minutes of a chess match on the fly, Bowden proved himself the offensive equal of the best mind in the college game, a play-calling artist named Steve Spurrier. I believe the sad asterisk on the best day of quarterback Stan White's long-and-winding football life is the realization that four years of work under Bowden could have made him the equal of the Shulers and the Zeiers.

I believe that the best 1-2 punch in college football may be Terry Bowden and Wayne Hall, the new offensive mastermind and the old defensive warhorse. I believe that on a day his undermanned, overmatched defense allowed 560 yards and 27 first downs and 35 points, Hall did some of his finest work in keeping his team in the game.

I believe the strength it took to come from-behind to beat Florida, to stand firm in the face of the furious Florida offense, was forged over the course of the first six games as the players and coaches discovered that Bowden knows whereof he speaks when the subject is college football, and that Bowden belongs right here.

THEY CAN BEAT BAMA

I believe any team that can surrender 560 yards and 35 points to Florida and not surrender can go undefeated. I believe it is time to speak the previously unspeakable, and it is time to believe that Auburn can beat Alabama.

I believe one man can make a difference, and Bowden has made all the difference, with his knowledge and his work and his heart, the one still pounding late Saturday afternoon under his raindrenched, sweat-soaked shirt.

I believe that on some distant day when probation is nothing more than a bad dream, Bowden and Spurrier will dance this dance again in the pale moonlight of Legion Field on the first Saturday in December.

I believe Pat Dye, as happy as a former football coach can be watching players he nurtured reach heights they never reached under his hand, wrote the perfect ending to the day that crossed the bridge from the past. I believe Dye spoke from the heart when he said, "Terry will have a lot of big wins. The great thing in our situation is Terry is 37 years old. He'll be here a long time."

Florida coach Steve Spurrier's face tells the story of his team's predicament with Auburn.
Joe Songer photo

Florida runners fought for yardage but gang-tackling Auburn defenders won the day.
Hal Yeager photo

Dye's post-game visit

Former Auburn coach Pat Dye paid his first postgame victory trip to the Tigers locker room after Saturday's victory over Florida.

"I've been pulling for this football team, the players and the coaches," said Dye. "I'm so thankful and happy for them that they have an opportunity to experience some success. They hadn't been able to do that in the last few years, and it wasn't their fault."

As for the Tigers' performance on the field, Dye said, "They did what they had to do to win. It wasn't easy. They didn't turn the football over. They had a good kicking game.

"Florida's got a great offensive football team and had Auburn outmatched in places when they went to three and four wide receivers. That caused them to give up a lot of easy yardage to (running back Errict) Rhett

that made it look worse than it really was. The difference in the two halves was when they stopped Rhett from running the football and Florida couldn't sustain a drive."

—*Neal Sims*

White sets record

Quarterback Stan White became Auburn's all-time offensive leader Saturday. The record-breaking play came quickly, on Auburn's first offensive snap of the game.

White, who needed just 5 yards coming in to move ahead of Pat Sullivan in career total offense, got it with a 16-yard sideline pass to wide receiver Thomas Bailey.

White finished the day with 280 total yards, 267 passing and 13 rushing, giving him 7,119 career yards in his fourth season as the starting quarterback. Sullivan, playing only three seasons at a time when freshmen were ineligible, had 6,843 total yards in his career.

—*Neal Sims*

Tigers leap nine spots in AP poll

The Associated Press

Auburn started out the season as an average football team in the eyes of coach Terry Bowden.

"I figure the worst thing you can call somebody is average," Bowden said before the first game, "but that's what we are."

Seven weeks later, he has raised his expectations.

"We're good enough to beat a top four team," Bowden said after the Tigers did just that, upsetting Florida 38-35 Saturday. "I'm not going to say we're a top four team, but this team is good enough to beat a lot of football teams."

Auburn (7-0) is not a top four team— yet— but the Tigers did make the biggest jump in Sunday's Associated Press media poll, moving up from No. 19 to No. 10.

It's the Tigers' first appearance in the Top 10 since November 1990, when they plummeted from fourth to 15th after a 48-7 defeat at Florida.

Ironically, it was that game that signalled a change in fortunes for Auburn after three straight Southeastern Conference titles. The Tigers lost three of their final five games that

Joyous Auburn players swarm the field, reveling in the hard-earned victory. From left, Shannon Robique (56), Ben Williamson (19), and Tony Richardson (40).
Steve Barnette photo

An emotion-filled—and about-to-be drenched Terry Bowden—hugs one of his team's leaders, Reid McMilion. Frank Sanders wields the water cooler as Stan White (11), Patrick Nix (10) and Derrick Robinson (58) rush to join the fun.
Steve Barnette photo

season and went 5-6 and 5-5-1 the next two years.

Now, another Florida game had proved to be a landmark for the Auburn program.

"All I can say is it's a big day for Auburn," Bowden said. "A big day for our team. A big day for our program. A big day for our fans."

It was the kind of day that many players were expecting when they signed with the Tigers.

"This is the one reason I came to Auburn," said junior receiver Thomas Bailey. "This is old Auburn football, and I'm glad it's back. It was the biggest win of my life."

Bowden: "Auburn is back"

Neal Sims News staff writer

AUBURN—The question put to Auburn coach Terry Bowden was short and direct: Is Auburn back?

His answer was equally candid: "I believe Auburn is back."

Then he asked his own questions and gave his own answers. "Are we back to the top right now? Are we as talented as we have been in the past? No, but we're back on our way. We need to continue to improve and develop our program, but the direction we are heading is clear to us and clear to those who follow Auburn."

The glow continues for Bowden and his Tigers, who are off to a perfect start in their new coach's first season.

No. 9 Auburn (7-0 overall, 5-0 in the Southeastern Conference) resumes play at Arkansas (3-4, 2-3), kicking off at 2 p.m. Saturday at Razorback Stadium in Fayetteville. Meanwhile, Bowden has had to deal with the spotlight and the accelerating expectations of Auburn followers.

He addressed those topics Tuesday. "I have enough background to respect how temporary all the praise and adulation can be," he said, "to accept it while it's here and to know that the first time you lose a game that everyone expects you to win, the same people that are praising you will be asking what happened. I've got a little understanding. Those things come and go.

"My interest is for the long-term goals of this program on a continual basis, year-to-year," he added. "I have nowhere else to go. It's not win now, get something and jump up so I can go somewhere else. We're looking long-term."

The national notice given to Auburn's surprising season has its price and its rewards, especially in a year where the program, on NCAA probation, finds exposure hard to come by out of the South.

"It's a lot more demanding on my time than my players," said Bowden. "It's something that I have not experienced previously. It's been a little bit taxing. But without TV games, the print media has been critical in news coverage to keep Auburn out there in the public view. From the recruiting standpoint and exposure for our program, this is exactly what we needed."

It's paying off, he said.

"You can hear at night when you're on the phones to the recruits," said Bowden. "You can see the positive effect it is having."

The players and coaches have the situation in perspective, Bowden said.

"Some of our fans say, 'Bring on Alabama.' That's kind of normal, I think, for Auburn and Alabama. That's the way fans get. It's also pretty normal for the coaches not to get caught up in that," he said.

"Just look at our football team. It's not a team on paper, or even in their minds, dominant over anybody that we've played. Our players know that.

"We're very proud of our ranking. It's one of the few things we've got, other than our record, that our players can have because there's not something after the season for us. We'd like to hold onto it.

"We still have a ways to go to be as talented as a lot of teams in our conference. I'm not sure we're as talented as all of our opponents, but we are playing well enough to play with most people in our conference.

"We're a solid football team that is playing very well and very hard. We know we have to play hard and win close ballgames. We're the type of team that has to play with emotion, that has to expect a 60-minute ballgame. I think we're a top 10 team because of how we play, not because of special talents of our football team.

"Everybody's locked in on that belief. I don't think there's any doubt. There's not enough pro scouts standing around here telling our guys how good they are. We don't have agents trying to sneak around like they do when you've got four first-round draft picks."

Tailback James Bostic said the players see it like that, too.

"We can't go to a bowl game. About the only thing we've got going for us is moving up in these polls," said Bostic. "That's our goal this year, get Auburn back on the map."

Fans cheer their heroes as they head to the locker room; linebacker Terry Solomon, arms extended acknowledges the fans.
Steve Barnette photo

Florida	10	17	0	8	—35
Auburn	7	7	7	17	—38

First Quarter

Fla—FG Davis 49

Fla—Jackson 50 pass from Wuerffel (Davis kick)

Aub—C.Jackson 96 interception return (Etheridge kick)

Second Quarter

Aub—White 2 run (Etheridge kick)

Fla—FG Davis 36

Fla—Rhett 24 run (Davis kick)

Fla—Hill 23 pass from Wuerffel (Davis kick)

Third Quarter

Aub—Richardson 23 pass from White (Etheridge kick)

Fourth Quarter

Aub—Bostic 4 run (Etheridge kick)

Aub—Sanders 9 run (Etheridge kick)

Fla—Jackson 13 pass from Wuerffel (Jackson pass from Wuerffel)

Aub—FG Etheridge 41

Attendance— 85,214

	Fla	Aub
First downs	27	23
Rushes-yards	27-174	33-116
Passing	386	267
Return Yards	8	184
Comp-Att-Int	25-50-2	23-36-2
Punts	4-46	5-52
Fumbles-Lost	1-1	1-0
Penalties-Yards	**8-75**	**7-80**
Time of Possession	30:20	29:40

INDIVIDUALS
FLORIDA
Rushing

Player	Att.	Yds.	TD	Long
Wuerffel	4	-24	0	3
Rhett	22	196	1	38
Randolph	1	2	0	2

Passing

Player	A-C-I	Yds	TD	Long
Wuerffel	50-25-2	386	3	60

Receiving

Player	No.	Yds	TD	Long
Houston	2	30	0	21
Randolph	2	23	0	18
J.Jackson	3	108	2	60
W.Jackson	8	86	0	27
Doering	6	64	0	23
Rhett	2	45	0	37
Hill	1	23	1	23
Dean	1	7	0	7

Punting

Player	No.	Yds	Avg	Long
Edge	4	185	45.7	56

Returns

Player	Punts	Kickoff	Int.
Houston		1-23	

J.Jackson		3-51
Kennedy		2-8

AUBURN
Rushing

Player	Att.	Yds.	TD	Long
White	12	18	1	11
Bostic	17	76	1	16
Richardson	2	2	0	2
Sanders	2	25	1	16

Passing

Player	A-C-I	Yds	TD	Long
White	35-23-0	267	1	23
Sanders	1-0-0	0	0	0

Receiving

Player	No.	Yds	TD	Long
Bailey	6	91	0	20
Davis	4	30	0	11
Bostic	3	25	0	19
Sanders	5	64	0	16
Richardson	4	51	1	23
Dorn	1	6	0	6

Punting

Player	No.	Yds	Avg	Long
Daniel	5	262	52.4	71

Returns

Player	Punts	Kickoff	Int.
Bailey	2-23	6-121	
Shelling			1-65
C.Jackson			1-96

DEFENSE
FLORIDA

Tackles, assists —Kennedy 5-2; Wright 2-1; Lott 1-2; Hanks 9-1; Edge 1-0; Lake 4-0; Malone 2-0; Gilmore 1-4; Robinson 5-3; Hambrick 5-2; Bates 1-0; Carter 5-1; Monk 1-1; McMillian 2-1; Johnson 2-2; Campbell 2-0; Barnard 2-1; Church 1-2; McCorkle 1-0; Dean 0-1; W.Jackson 1-0.

Sacks —Gaines, Campbell. **Fumbles recovered** —None. **Passes intercepted** —None. **Passes broken up** — Gilmore.

AUBURN

Tackles, assists —Mounds 2-2; Shelling 6-3; Jackson 2-0; Robinson 7-4; Pina 2-0; McGee 5-0; Solomon 6-2; Miska 2-4; Pelton 2-2; Harris 6-4; Thornton 0-1; Whitehead 3-4; Miller 3-3; Walker 1-1; Hart 1-1; A.Etheridge 1-4; Frazier 2-0; Malcom 1-1; Clarke 1-0; Atkins 2-3.

Sacks —Atkins, Pelton. **Fumbles recovered** —Bailey, Crook. **Passes intercepted** —Jackson, Shelling. **Passes broken up** —McGee, Mounds, Jackson, B.Robinson.

AUBURN SEASON
Results (7-0)

Sept. 2	Ole Miss,	Won 16-12
Sept. 11	Samford,	Won 35-7
Sept. 18	at LSU,	Won 34-10
Sept. 25	Southern Miss,	Won 35-24
Oct. 2	at Vandy,	Won 14-10
Oct. 9	Miss. State,	Won 31-17
Oct. 16	Florida,	Won 38-35
Oct. 30	at Arkansas	
Nov. 6	New Mexico St.	
Nov. 13	at Georgia	
Nov. 20	Alabama	

A freak fall storm brought snow to Arkansas and heavy winter gear for coaches and players.
Steve Barnette photo

KEEPING WARM
Arkansas

Auburn puts freeze on Hogs; Tigers run their record to perfect 8-0

Neal Sims, News staff writer

FAYETTEVILLE, Ark.—Auburn shivered, Auburn shuddered, then Auburn knocked Arkansas cold on the frosty turf of Razorback Stadium Saturday.

The icy Tigers brought home the bacon, smoking the Hogs 31-21 and preserving the remarkable story of their still-perfect season under new coach Terry Bowden.

A thoroughly chilled Arkansas homecoming crowd of 50,100 saw Auburn stumble into the deep-freeze, then recover with a big second half built around a pass interception for a touchdown, Reid McMilion's double-steal of a fumble and McMilion's hard-charging runs that ground up the Razorbacks.

Ninth-ranked Auburn (8-0 overall, 6-0 in the Southeastern Conference), with a scoring blitz put together in the snow flurries and 10-degree wind-

The field may have been frosty, but Auburn's defense was hot as Willie Whitehead (90) and Randy Hart (98) crush the Arkansas ball carrier.
Steve Barnette photo

chill, was too much for Arkansas (3-5, 2-4) to overcome.

"I knew we were going to be in for a war," said Auburn coach Terry Bowden. "They were playing the same way we've been playing to win—play it close to the vest, play it to the end, but our guys have been getting pretty good at it."

Arkansas coach Danny Ford said, "Our team tried. We gave good effort. Our fans hung in there on a very cold day. I'm sorry it wasn't a better homecoming." The teams went to halftime tied 7-7. The Razorbacks had scored on a 76-yard drive the first time they had the ball, and the Tigers answered with a 56-yard pass from quarterback Stan White to wide receiver Frank Sanders that set up an Auburn touchdown.

But Auburn had missed other opportunities, and that had Bowden concerned. "It was a dangerous game," he said.

The Tigers had missed two field goals, one when Scott Etheridge's 40-yard attempt was driven into the turf by the stiff wind and another when holder Sean Carder dropped the snap.

Etheridge saved that from being an Arkansas return for a touchdown with his tackle. "Any time I'm on the defensive stats," he said, "it's obviously not good.

"Kicking in the wind is not easy," added Etheridge, "but the balls are just absolute bricks in the cold."

Said Bowden, "We were doing just enough to get beat." So at halftime, he said, "I asked our guys

Quarterback Stan White got good protection and led the Tigers to a 31-point performance. Here White operates behind the protection of guard Todd Boland (52) and tight end Andy Fuller (82).
Frank Couch photo

to make a big play, somebody make a big play. Brian Robinson made it. Then we were one step ahead of 'em from that point."

Robinson delivered on his coach's call almost immediately. With barely a minute played in the third quarter, he picked off a pass when Arkansas tight end Kirk Botkin slipped while the ball was in the air and ran 35 yards with his interception for a touchdown.

"That turned around the game," said Bowden.

Said Robinson, "I thought I could provide a spark, and I did."

Sanders, who had seven catches for 134 yards, made another big one, a leaping grab for a 32-yard gain, to set up Auburn's next score. But first came the double-fumble. Tigers tailback James Bostic

lost the ball, and the Razorbacks' Alfred Jackson recovered. "He picked it up," said Auburn's McMilion, "and I just happened to be right there beside him. He was kind of holding it funny, so I just reached out there, grabbed it and took it away from him. The ref was right there and saw everything."

That saved Etheridge a shot at a 37-yard field goal to put Auburn up 17-7.

Arkansas closed with a 50-yard bomb from quarterback Barry Lunney to split end J.J. Meadors, but was shut down from then on by the Auburn defense until the game was safely put away.

The Tigers chewed up the rest of the third quarter with a 68-yard drive that ended with

Incredible Tigers could win 'em all

Jimmy Bryan, News staff writer

FAYETTEVILLE, Ark.—Put 'em in the smothering heat of early September or a snowringed deep freeze in the closing days of October, and Auburn simply shrugs and bashes another head.

Auburn put its eighth win of the season away Saturday, 31-21 over the Arkansas Razorbacks as snowflakes floated on a freezing wind. The wind had what is called "wind chill factor" at 10 degrees when the game kicked off. It was probably like zero when it finished.

With New Mexico State coming to Auburn Saturday, you can go ahead and ring up at least a 9-win season. A win over Georgia or Alabama closing up would bring double figure wins. Who expected that?

For a team on probation, with no bowl and no television to showcase this incredible run under first-year coach Terry Bowden, the Tigers are running on talent with a lot of pride.

There is precedent for what the Tigers are getting done in the face of probation. The 1957 Auburn team won a national championship despite sanctions, and the 1975 Oklahoma team did the same.

Florida would have won the SEC champi-

onship with a 6-1 league mark and 9-2 overall record in 1990 but was on probation. The Gators had 9-1-1 records in 1984 and '85, but got no championships. These teams were on probation, too.

The current Arkansas coach, Danny Ford, had a couple of 9-1-1 seasons at Clemson when those Tigers were on probation from '82 to '84. Now Bowden and the Tigers are getting perfect results despite probation.

What gives? Ford has a pretty good answer.

"You take an us-against-the-world attitude and get your team closer and closer together," Ford said.

Bowden has given Stan White back the confidence he lost the last two years when there was no rhythm to the offense. People forget how efficient White was when Pat Sullivan brought him along during a redshirt year ('89) and an outstanding freshman season.

They forget he brought Auburn back from a 19-point deficit to tie Tennessee 26-26 and rallied the Tigers in the fourth quarter to beat Florida State 20-17 in 1990.

Now they're seeing Stan the Man again. And they are seeing an Auburn team that might win 'em all.

Bostic's touchdown on the first play of the final period. Then Auburn upped it to 31-14 with a 58-yard drive that saw McMilion carry the ball on five of the six plays.

"We got down there in the fourth quarter," said McMilion, "and it was just like we're going to run right at you. You stop us if you can, and they never could.

"The holes were huge. It was wide open. When they're blocking like that, if you can't get five and six yards, you don't even need to be running the ball. Everything was like it used to be. It felt like old times."

The Hogs cut the score to the final margin with a late drive for a touchdown.

As for the weather, Bowden said, "It was awful. It was tough on both teams.

"It's kind of a macho thing. Who's going to pretend it doesn't affect you? But when you walk out there, all you think about is how cold you are. It was a factor.

"But," he added, "the show is always somewhere. Wherever you've got to play, you've got to play. You disregard the weather, the elements and the circumstances. That's what it takes to be in the show."

McMilion chokes hogs, then chokes up himself

Neal Sims, News staff writer

FAYETTEVILLE, Ark.—Off in the corner of the tiny blue-and-white tent, the television cameras gone from his postgame interview session, Auburn fullback Reid McMilion couldn't keep his emotions checked any longer.

He had choked the Arkansas Razorbacks with his rugged running, burying their hopes time and again with big carries through the middle of the Hogs defense, then he choked up himself.

McMilion's thoughts turned from his Saturday feats to his five years at Auburn—his knee surgeries, his comebacks, his decision to stay when he was close to giving it up— and he let a tear or two of joy and recaptured pride escape from his eyes.

"I about started crying," said McMilion, and he did. "I didn't know if I was going to be back. I finally proved it to myself. This meant a lot.

"It's been a hard road, but I think it's going to pay off. It's paid off already. It's been an outstanding season. It's been a lot of fun, and it's not over yet."

McMilion, who sat out spring recovering from knee surgery, turned in his best game of the season Saturday, rushing for 91 yards and scoring the Tigers' final touchdown in Auburn's 31-21 victory over Arkansas.

"I was waiting for Reid to show up," said McMilion of himself, "and he actually showed up.

"I had a lot of doubts," he acknowledged. "A

lot of times, I felt like I didn't need to be out there. A lot of players went through a lot of things. There was a point in time when I was going to quit right before the season started, and the seniors held me together.

"I couldn't participate as much as I wanted to in practice," he recalled of the beginning of his final season at Auburn. "It was hard for my family and for me. It was hard for the guys to watch me. They knew I wanted to play the game and wanted to be out there with them. I'm glad I'm here.

"Once I got through the first game, I knew my place was to be on this team. If I couldn't be a leader on the field, I was going to be a leader off the field—before games, after games, halftime, there's a part I can play.

"It's all come down to this. Every bit of it has been worth it, the pain and the effort. I'm happy to be here with this senior class. They are the ones who inspired me and kept me here as a player."

Senior quarterback Stan White, McMilion's roommate for three years, reflected on his teammate's dilemma early this season. "Reid is such an emotional guy when it comes to big decisions like that," said White. "I told him, 'This is our last year. Think about it. If you don't play, you'll go out of here 5-5-1. You don't want that feeling.'

"I knew he wanted to contribute more and he didn't think he was. But he contributes by just being there."

THE YARDSTICK

Auburn	7	0	10	14 — 31
Arkansas	7	0	7	7 — 21

First Quarter
ARK—Malone 6 run (Boulware kick)

AU—White 1 run (Etheridge kick)

Third Quarter
AU—35 interception return (Etheridge kick)

AU—FG Etheridge 37

ARK—Meadors 50 pass from Lunney (Boulware kick)

Fourth Quarter
AU—Bostic 12 run (Etheridge kick)

AU—McMilion 16 run (Etheridge kick

ARK—Caldwell 16 pass form Lunney (Boulware kick)

Attendance— 50,100

	Auburn	Arkansas
First downs	25	19
Rushes-yards	47-247	32-95
Passing	212	286
Return Yards	35	15
Comp-Att-Int	15-26-1	17-41-1
Punts	2-48	4-40
Fumbles-Lost	3-3	1-1
Penalties-Yards	4-38	5-64
Time of Possession	34:03	25:57

INDIVIDUALS
AUBURN
Rushing

Player	Att.	Yds.	TD	Long
McMilion	12	91	1	21
Bostic	21	88	1	25
White	4	36	1	20
Richardson	4	27	0	19
Malcom	2	10	0	6
Morrow	2	10	0	6
Nix	1	1	0	1
Carder	1	-16	0	-16

Passing

Player	A-C-I	Yds	TD	Long
White	26-15-1	212	0	56

Receiving

Player	No.	Yds	TD	Long
Sanders	7	134	0	56
Richardson	3	38	0	19
Bailey	3	28	0	11
McMilion	2	12	0	13

Punting

Player	No.	Yds	Avg	Long
Daniel	2	95	47.5	48

Returns

Player	Punts	Kickoff	Int.
Bailey		5-66	
B.Robinson			1-35
Carder		1-0	

ARKANSAS
Rushing

Player	Att.	Yds.	TD	Long
Calvin	12	41	0	13
Malone	11	38	1	15
Lunney	6	11	0	17
Gray	1	7	0	7
Hebert	2	-2	0	1

Passing

Player	A-C-I	Yds	TD	Long
Lunney	41-17-1	286	2	50

Receiving

Player	No.	Yds	TD	Long
Meadors	3	72	1	50
Botkin	4	71	0	42
Caldwell	3	42	1	16
Malone	1	40	0	40
Perry	3	25	0	11
Gray	2	24	0	18
M.Johnson	1	12	0	12

Punting

Player	No.	Yds	Avg	Long
Preston	4	160	40	57

Returns

Player	Punts	Kickoff	Int.
Watters	2-11	5-102	
Kidd			0-1

DEFENSE
AUBURN
Tackles, assists —Mounds 2-3; Shelling 3-1; Frazier 2-2; Jackson 3-2; Johnson 2-1; B. Robinson 3-2; McGee 1-0; Crook 0-2; Solomon 1-1; Miska 6-8; Pelton 0-3; A. Harris 3-4; Primus 2-1; Whitehead 0-1; A. Etheridge 0-2; Hart 1-3; Atkins 0-1; Malcom 0-1; Waller 0-1; Morrow 0-1.

Sacks —Pelton, A.Harris 2. **Fumbles recovered** —McMilion. **Passes intercepted** —B.Robinson. **Passes broken up** — A.Harris, Whitehead.

ARKANSAS
Tackles, assists —Kidd 0-4; Watters 1-2; Hicks 2-0; Ireland 2-14; Cantlope 5-2; Nunnerly 0-1; A.Jackson 2-1; W.Johnson 0-5; M.Smith 1-1; Chatman 1-5; M.Adair 1-6; Knap 1-11; Wishon 3-1; Bell 1-2; Ford 2-4; Wade 0-5; Conley 0-1; Kinnebrew 0-1; Thomas 1-1.

Sacks —None. **Fumbles recovered** —Kidd, Hicks. **Passes intercepted** —Watters. **Passes broken up** —Cantlope, M.Smith.

AUBURN SEASON
Results (8-0)

Sept. 2	Ole Miss,	Won 16-12
Sept. 11	Samford,	Won 35-7
Sept. 18	at LSU,	Won 34-10
Sept. 25	Southern Miss,	Won 35-24
Oct. 2	at Vandy,	Won 14-10
Oct. 9	Miss. State,	Won 31-17
Oct. 16	Florida,	Won 38-35
Oct. 30	at Arkansas,	Won 31-21
Nov. 6	New Mexico St.	
Nov. 13	at Georgia	
Nov. 20	Alabama	

Linebacker Jason Miska and other Auburn defensemen have a big day against New Mexico State
Mark Almond photo

A FINAL TUNE-UP
New Mexico State

AU eyes higher ranking after rout

Neal Sims, News staff writer

AUBURN—New Mexico State won the first quarter of Auburn's homecoming game Saturday, but that registers barely a blip in the Aggies' memory after what came next. Auburn won everything else, walloping the Aggies 55-14 and burying their outmanned opponents under a scoring onslaught. "We could do pretty much what we needed to do," said Auburn coach Terry Bowden, whose team at one point scored on eight straight possessions, including five second-quarter touchdowns. "There was not much mystery after a quarter. It was over at the half."

New Mexico State coach Jim Hess looked at the mismatch philosophically. "They got what they wanted—an easy homecoming win. We got what we wanted—the money," said Hess who brought his team from the Big West Conference to play before 82,128 fans at Jordan-Hare Stadium, the largest crowd ever to see a New Mexico State football game.

"He was right," agreed Bowden. "We were too strong for them. There's a difference in the two levels of play. It was clear and evident."

Auburn (9-0 overall, 6-0 in the Southeastern Conference) used more than 70 players, including three quarterbacks, eight running backs and 13 receivers, to gun down New Mexico State (5-4, 4-1 and leading the Big West). The ample margin of victory, plus some churning among other top 10 teams Saturday, is almost certain to send the No. 8 Tigers higher in the national rankings this week.

"As long as they keep us up there, you never know what's going to happen," said Bowden. "We kept ourselves 9-0 going to Georgia with a chance to be 10-0."

Particularly impressive Saturday was Stan White. The Auburn quarterback completed 19 of his 22 passes in the first half, and two of the three misses were drops. At one point, White hit 16 straight, an Auburn record. Bowden labeled the performance "magnificent."

"Stan White had a phenomenal day," he said. "You have to know who the receivers were and who he hit to understand the day he had. He was going down to second and third receivers."

White played only five minutes into the third quarter before giving way to backups and finished with 23 of 30 passing for 248 yards and three touchdowns.

The Aggies looked almost dangerous early. On the second snap of the game, wideout Kenny Canady was open deep when Auburn defensive back Dell McGee fell down, but the freshman dropped what would have been a 76-yard touchdown pass.

The Aggies did get on the board after Auburn tailback James Bostic fumbled at the Tigers' 29-yard line. Quarterback Cody Ledbetter put New Mexico State ahead 7-0 when he rolled right and scored from 3 yards out.

"We had some adversity," said Bowden. "We turned the ball over. They got a touchdown. It put a little scare in me. I was proud to see it quickly turned back the other way and then not slow down."

Auburn charged back. White completed 5 of 5 passes on a drive that stalled on running plays at the New Mexico State 10. Scott Etheridge's 27-yard field goal made it 7-3.

Then the Tigers posted three quick touchdowns. A 50-yard drive took only four plays, with fullback Tony Richardson bursting through the middle for a 24-yard score. A 60-yard drive took three plays. Tailback Stephen Davis ran for 35 yards, and wideout Thomas Bailey scored on a 23-yard catch, beating a defender inside the 5 and lunging into the end zone.

"I had to get inside him, and Stan did a great

job of leading me out," said Bailey. "After I caught it, I was determined to get the touchdown."

Then came another 50-yard drive, this one also in three plays. Bostic's 38-yard run set up the score, another power run up the middle by Richardson.

Both of his touchdowns were on the same call, said Richardson, a misdirection play that turns into a fullback dive.

"We have so much success running the sweep to the outside with Bostic," he said, "they just load everybody up outside and the inside is open."

The Tigers made it 31-7 on a touchdown pass from White to Bostic, the tailback's first scoring catch this season.

"Most of the time, everybody sees me on the run," said Bostic. "They get used to that. This time, I was in for the pass."

A 17-yard touchdown pass from White to wide receiver Frank Sanders closed the first-half scoring at 38-3.

"They really could not stop the things we were doing. We were making big, big yardage," said Bowden, who even brought all his offensive assistants down from the press box to the sidelines for the second half.

The Tigers took the second-half kickoff and marched to Etheridge's second field goal. That was it for White.

Quarterback Patrick Nix directed the next touchdown drive, and after the Aggies scored again, third-team quarterback Patrick Sullivan directed the final scoring march. Both TDs came from third-team tailback Roymon Malcolm, the last one on a fourth-down play with 40 seconds to play.

"We had third-teamers in there, and they wanted to score," said Bowden. "We'd have had to sit on it a long time. I don't think anybody was upset."

Hess wasn't. "We were just worn out. Terry wasn't trying to run up the score."

Auburn fullback and team leader Reid McMilion pours it on outmanned New Mexico State.
Mark Almond photo

Auburn on the move

Auburn entered Saturday No. 8 in the Associated Press poll, but the way the day unfolded, the Tigers could find themselves much higher come Monday morning.

No. 3 Ohio State tied Wisconsin. No. 5 Alabama lost to LSU. No. 6 Nebraska barely squeaked by Kansas by a point.

"We look for any circumstances that will move us up in the polls," Auburn coach Terry Bowden said. "The AP poll is all we got right now as far as outside. We want to win every game, but our little fun thing is that AP poll. There's really not a big chance that they're going to name us national champions, but the AP poll, as long as they keep us up there, you never know what's going to happen.

"The poll is what keeps us motivated. It's a little more motivation for us. Of course, at this point you don't really need any more motivation."

—*Kevin Scarbinsky*

Win, as usual

Auburn observed its 67th homecoming football game the way it usually does—with a victory.

The Tigers' 55-14 drubbing of New Mexico State marked the 54th time Auburn has beaten its homecoming guests. Auburn's overall record in homecoming games is now 54-9-4.

— *Neal Sims*

Bostic may fumble away job

Coach Terry Bowden continues to be upset with tailback James Bostic's disturbing habit of losing the football. Bostic fumbled on his first carry Saturday, setting up the Aggies for a touchdown at the Tigers' 29-yard line.

After the game, Bowden said he's considering starting Stephen Davis against Georgia rather than risk possible fumbles from Bostic, the No.2 rusher in the Southeastern Conference.

"The Bostic story hasn't changed," said Bowden. "I'm upset. I'm disappointed. We've got to solve it, or it's going to cost us a ballgame.

"If we can't correct it, we've got to decide whether we want to go into a game against Georgia with a high percentage that he's going to fumble. It scares me."

Bowden noted that Bostic, too, was disturbed by the problem. "You can't write anything or say anything that will make him more disappointed. He's working hard."

Bostic ran for 104 yards Saturday and scored a touchdown, his first on a catch this season. "I don't know what the problem is," he said of the fumbling, "but I'll have it corrected before the Georgia game. It hurts the team. It's something I've got to control."

—*Neal Sims*

Bowden: "We best think of Ga."

Neal Sims, News staff writer

AUBURN—Some Auburn followers are ready to say it. The Associated Press poll voters already have. But to those who say the football fortunes have flipped for this state's two major college teams, Auburn coach Terry Bowden has this reply:

"I would say they've jumped the gun."

Few would have believed it 10 weeks ago, but today Auburn is the highest ranked team from this state, checking in with a perfect record at No. 7 in the AP's top 25, five notches ahead of defending national champion Alabama.

But Bowden said Sunday he's taking no personal satisfaction in that standing just yet.

"We've all got two more games in the season," he said. "Just when you start feeling real good about yourself, somebody is good enough to come up and knock you off. Just when you start gloating is when you get knocked off. We best just think of Georgia."

Auburn (9-0 overall, 6-0 in the Southeastern Conference) heads for Georgia (4-5, 2-5) this week before closing out the season against Alabama.

"We're proud that they picked us No. 7," said Bowden of this week's poll. "It's a step up. We've been using that as motivation all year. But now that we're to Georgia, you really don't need any of that. We're going to be motivated for Georgia. The polls can take a back seat now. All the motivation is over at Athens.

"They quite possibly are the hottest team in the conference," Bowden added of the Bulldogs, who have won three of their last four games after a horrendous start. "They have made the biggest move. You can't look at Georgia's record. You've got to look at what they're doing the last few games. Because of what they're doing offensively—throwing the football with (quarterback

Eric) Zeier—they've become a new team. They're probably good enough right now to beat anybody in the conference."

Bowden said the Bulldogs have a decided advantage coming into the Auburn game with a week off. "We have to anticipate a scoring match with Georgia," he said. "Somehow, we have to find ways to be productive."

The Tigers were plenty productive Saturday, rolling up 579 yards of offense in a 55-14 whipping of New Mexico State. That left Aggies coach Jim Hess wondering about the Tigers. "Who's to say they are not the best team in the nation?" he asked. "They're certainly playing great football right now. Auburn is a superbly coached team. There may be teams they play that have better players, but Auburn is playing offense, defense and kicking now about as well as you can play it.

"Auburn has a chance to go 11-0," he added. "I know I saw a very good team out there."

Bowden said, "I was extremely pleased with the way we played against New Mexico State—not because we had to play great to win. It was obvious after a little bit that we would probably win even if we played badly. That was not what we wanted to do.

"We really wanted our young men to come out and play their very best football and try to get better. If that allowed us to beat them badly, then that's what we wanted to do. If it would have been just enough to win, that would have been OK, too.

"The thing that I'm pleased most about is not the outcome, the score or the point spread, but that we were playing about as good as we could play. We looked very, very, good offensively and defensively—and very serious. There was no lackadaisical attitude or any complacency. That's what I wanted to see, some intensity."

NMex St.	7	0	7	0—14
Auburn	3	35	10	7—55

First Quarter
NMSU—Ledbetter 3 run (Culin kick)

Aub—FG Etheridge 27

Second Quarter
Aub—Richardson 21 run (Etheridge kick)

Aub—Bailey 23 pass from White (Etheridge kick)

Aub—Richardson 9 run (Etheridge kick)

Aub—Bostic 5 pass from White (Etheridge kick)

Aub—Sanders 17 pass from White (Etheridge kick)

Third Quarter
Aub—FG Etheridge 26

Aub—Malcolm 6 pass from Nix (Etheridge kick)

Fourth Quarter
NMSU—Suttles 8 pass from Ledbetter (Culin kick)

Aub—Malcolm 1 run (Etheridge kick)

Attendance— 82,128

	NMSU	Aub
First downs	8	31
Rushes-yards	24-81	46-289
Passing	113	290
Return Yards	0	65
Comp-Att-Int	11-24-1	28-40-0
Punts	9-36	3-42
Fumbles-Lost	1-0	1-1
Penalties-Yards	**4-28**	**7-63**
Time of Possession	23:49	36:11

INDIVIDUALS
NEW MEXICO ST.
Rushing
Player	Att.	Yds.	TD	Long
Ledbetter	5	-11	1	3
Dublin	14	59	0	11
Dizula	4	30	0	24
Miller	1	3	0	3

Passing
Player	A-C-I	Yds	TD	Long
Ledbetter	24-11-1	113	1	35

Receiving
Player	No.	Yds	TD	Long
Laing	2	31	0	19
Osborne	3	15	0	8
Pizula	2	5	0	3
Davis	1	35	0	35
Canaday	2	19	0	12
Suttles	1	8	1	8

Punting
Player	No.	Yds	Avg	Long
Zecha	9	320	35.5	42

Returns
Player	Punts	Kickoff	Int.
Foster		4-113	
Banks		2-48	

AUBURN
Rushing
Player	Att.	Yds.	TD	Long
White	4	18	0	16
McMilion	3	20	0	15
Bostic	11	104	0	38
Davis	5	13	0	5
Richardson	2	30	2	21
Sanders	1	11	0	11
Malcom	10	76	1	18
Morrow	7	17	0	6
Nix	1	-2	0	-2
Sullivan	1	1	0	1

Passing
Player	A-C-I	Yds	TD	Long
White	30-23-0	248	3	35
Nix	9-5-0	42	1	12
Sullivan	1-0-0	0	0	0

Receiving
Player	No.	Yds	TD	Long
Carder	6	62	0	17
Sanders	4	48	1	17
McMilion	1	3	0	3
Bailey	2	29	1	23
Dorn	4	40	0	20
Davis	2	40	0	35
Bostic	2	5	1	5
Richardson	2	21	0	18
Davidson	1	8	0	8
Gosha	1	12	0	12

Punting
Player	No.	Yds	Avg	Long
Daniel	3	126	42	50

Returns
Player	Punts	Kickoff	Int.
Bailey	4-34	2-51	
Shelling			1-31

DEFENSE
FLORIDA
Tackles, assists — Frazier 1-0; Rowser 4-3; Barela 2-0; Stowers 7-2; Walton 9-0; Manuel 4-0; LeBreton 5-1; Gray 6-2; Wall 3-0; Melendez 3-0; Mauck 6-2; Takapu 1-0; Poznich 2-1; Wade 2-1; Duplessis 1-1; LaChapelle 1-1; Woods 1-0; Kern 1-0; Beene 5-0; Johnson 1-0; Pizula 1-0; McIntyre 1-0; Foster 1-1; Modzeiewski 0-1.

Sacks — Melendez, Manuel, LeBreton. Fumbles recovered — Walton. Passes intercepted — None. Passes broken up — Manuel 2.

AUBURN
Tackles, assists — Mounds 3-1; Shelling 4-3; Jackson 1-0; Johnson 0-1; Robinson 0-2; McGee 3-1; Miska 1-4; Pelton 3-0; Harris 4-0; Thornton 3-1; Robinson 1-1; Primus 2-1; Whitehead 1-3; Luster 0-1; Miller 0-2; Walker 2-0; Hart 1-1; Etheridge 3-0; Frazier 2-0; Morrow 1-0; Crook 1-0; Burton 2-0; Will 1-0.

Sacks — Walker, Pelton. Fumbles recovered — None. Passes intercepted — Shelling. Passes broken up — Mounds, Shelling, Walker, Robinson.

AUBURN SEASON
Results (9-0)

Sept. 2	Ole Miss, Won 16-12
Sept. 11	Samford, Won 35-7
Sept. 18	at LSU, Won 34-10
Sept. 25	Southern Miss, Won 35-24
Oct. 2	at Vandy, Won 14-10
Oct. 9	Miss. State, Won 31-17
Oct. 16	Florida, Won 38-35
Oct. 30	at Arkansas, Won 31-21
Nov. 6	New Mexico St., Won 55-14
Nov. 13	at Georgia
Nov. 20	Alabama

Georgia's great quarterback Eric Zeier got his yards against Auburn, but it wasn't easy with Auburn defenders in his face all day.
Hal Yeager photo

AMEN, BROTHER
Georgia

"We're the best," Bowden declares, Auburn kicks dawgs, sets sights on Bama

Neal Sims, News staff writer

ATHENS, Ga.—Call 'em a perfect 10. The record does. Call 'em the best football team in the Southeastern Conference. Saturday, their coach finally said that out loud.

"The others can play in Birmingham for the SEC Championship," said Auburn coach Terry Bowden, "but on the field, this is the best team in the SEC."

So came the pronouncement from Bowden after Auburn adorned itself with what will be the best regular-season record in the SEC this year, outgunning Georgia 42-28 Saturday.

"As I told our players," said Bowden, "we've beaten everybody on the field. We've accomplished our next-to-last goal. Alabama is next, our last goal for the state championship."

Unbeaten and seventh-ranked Auburn (10-0 overall, 7-0 in the SEC) overwhelmed Georgia (4-6, 2-6) with its offense in the highest-scoring game ever in these two old rivals' 97-game history. The Tigers' defense couldn't shut out the Bulldogs and quarterback Eric Zeier, but it left him with little chance for a comeback in front of a Sanford Stadium sellout of 85,434.

James Bostic, on the sidelines at the start to settle his fumbling jitters, was the big gun, coming off the bench to run for 183 yards and score three touchdowns.

The Tigers' 10-0 start clinches the league's best record no matter what happens in their season-closer against Alabama this week. Florida is the only SEC team with no ties and only one loss, and that defeat was to Auburn.

"We became the best team in the SEC and in our minds," said Bowden. "They can't take that away from us."

Georgia coach Ray Goff, whose team came in with victories in three of its last four games, wasn't going to argue.

"They're undefeated," said Goff. "That's a pretty good indication they must be doing something right.

"We had an opportunity to play some good football," Goff added, "but they took advantage of some opportunities. We had our backs to the wall. After that, they knew what we were going to do every snap. We got down, and we had no choice but to throw."

Both sides piled up the offense in a game that saw more than 1,000 total yards and 70 points. Zeier threw 53 times, passing for 426 of Georgia's 508 yards. Behind Bostic, Auburn ran for 303 of its 495.

The Tigers shot out first, scoring on their opening drive. Tony Richardson broke a straight fullback dive up the middle for a 28-yard touchdown run.

"We knew they would try to load up the end to stop the sweep," said Richardson. "It was wide open. I hit the hole and scored."

A punt penned Georgia back at its own 6, but the Dogs didn't mind. They marched the distance. A 37-yard run by scatback Terrell Davis set up the score, and he got the TD to make it 7-7.

But the Dogs were out of it before they could score again.

On a third-and-two play, with the Georgia defense stacking the line, Bostic slammed through the left side and was gone, 41 yards for the score. "We were using two tight ends, and they were in a goal-line defense," said Bostic. "Once I broke free, it was

Georgia ball carriers were   harrassed throughout the day.
Steve Barnette photo

wide open and a touchdown. If they had caught me, we'd have got it in one way or the other."

The Tigers almost blew their next scoring chance, but the Bulldogs gave then a second chance.

Defensive end Andre Miller wrecked a Georgia reverse, and several Auburn defenders chased the ball back to the 18 but were unable to hold on. The Dogs lost 25 yards but not the ball. They lost that on the next snap, a fumble recovered by Calvin Jackson.

Bostic took a toss sweep left, then it cut it back inside for his second touchdown and a 21-7 Auburn lead at the half.

The teams swapped back-to-back scores in the third period. Auburn made it 28-7 on a 73-yard pass interception return by cornerback Chris Shelling. He snared a tipped ball, raced across the field and down the sideline for the TD. Bowden, leaping and shouting along the way, came closest to catching him.

Shelling described his moment. "We had a blitz called. We showed it early, Zeier checked off and Brian Robinson recognized it. He backed up and batted the ball. I broke up on the ball and took off with it. I kept heading for the corner to stay ahead of them. I think I ran about 130 yards because if I had stayed straight, one of their players would have caught me."

Georgia scored on the next play, a 76-yard bomb from Zeier to Hason Graham, but Auburn went into the final period up 35-14 after a TD pass from Stan White to Frank Sanders.

The teams exchanged two more scores to wrap it up. Bostic's 26-yard run on a toss sealed it.

Bostic big day, AU back rumbles for 183 yards, 3 tds— and no fumbles

Neal Sims, News staff writer

ATHENS, Ga.—Stephen Davis' backup had a big day for Auburn Saturday.

"That not starting must have ticked him off a little bit," said Davis, referring to his friend and running mate James Bostic, who missed most of the opening quarter, then went on a rampage in the Tigers' 42-28 victory over Georgia.

Bostic was on the sidelines at the start, a move that coach Terry Bowden figured was a solution to the tailback's tendency to fumble early in the game.

The plan worked. Bostic didn't fumble. He just ran and scored.

Bostic rushed for a season-high 183 yards, scored three touchdowns and went over the 1,000-yard mark for the year.

"He came in and played a great game," said Davis. "I'm proud of him."

Echoed Bowden. "What a day for James Bostic."

Bowden said he made the decision during the week to hold out Bostic but didn't tell him until during warmups.

"We held him out because of the fumbles," explained Bowden, "just to get the tension of the first series away, not for punishment."

Bostic did get in for two plays late in the first quarter, then took it to the Georgia defense. On a third-and-two play, Bostic ripped through the left side of the line and was gone on a 41-yard touchdown play. He added another touchdown in the first half, taking a toss pitch in from 3 yards away, then scored the game's final TD on a 26-yard run.

"I just had to do what I could once I got in there," said Bostic, adding that he wasn't upset over the coaching move to start him out on the sidelines.

"I knew Coach had to do something," said Bostic. "I couldn't get down because he did that. I'd dug myself in the hole. Once I got in there, I knew I had to play ball."

Bostic said, "The coaches told me to go ahead and take it like it was all behind me. I didn't think about it or worry about it. It was a big game, and I knew I had to do my share.

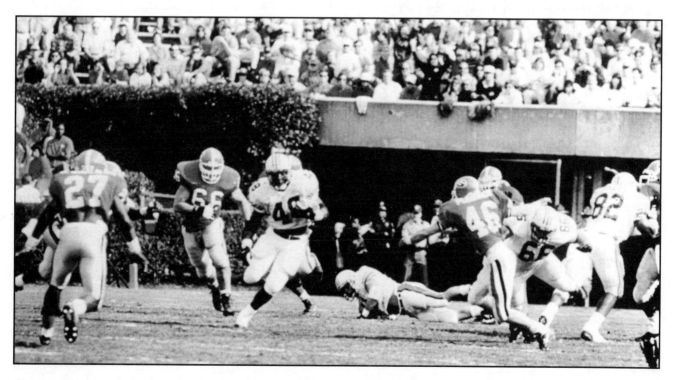

Stephen Davis sets sail with great line blocking through a huge hole in the Georgia defense.
Hal Yeager photo

"When I got out there, I wasn't going to be denied. I ran hard. The line blocked well. The fullbacks blocked. The holes were there. I had to take advantage of it."

Auburn by the numbers: last 10-0 record in '57

Some numbers to chew on from Auburn's 42-28 victory over Georgia:

This is the second time in Auburn history the Tigers have been 10-0. The first was when the 1957 national championship team finished the season with that mark.

Auburn's 42 points were the most points the Tigers have scored against Georgia since a 44-0 victory on Nov. 30, 1900, in Atlanta.

The two teams combined for 70 points, the highest-scoring game in the 97 meetings between Auburn and Georgia.

James Bostic's 183-yard rushing performance put him over 1,000 yards for the season, the sixth Auburn back to break that mark.

Wide receiver Frank Sanders became the 10th Auburn player to have 1,000 yards in career receptions.

Auburn	7	14	14	7	—42
Georgia	7	0	7	14	—28

First Quarter
Aub—Richardson 28 run (Etheridge kick)

Ga—T. Davis 1 run (Parkman kick)

Second Quarter
Aub—Bostic 41 run (Etheridge kick)

Aub—Bostic 3 run (Etheridge kick)

Third Quarter
Aub—Shelling 73 interception return (Etheridge kick)

Ga—Graham 76 pass from Zeier (Parkman kick)

Aub—Sanders 10 pass from White (Etheridge kick)

Fourth Quarter
Ga—Hunter 4 pass from Zeier (Parkman kick)

Ga—Bohannon 8 pass from Zeier (Parkman kick)

Aub—Bostic 26 run (Etheridge kick)

Attendance— 85,434

	Aub	Ga
First downs	24	27
Rushes-yards	45-303	35-82
Passing	192	426
Return Yards	80	46
Comp-Att-Int	16-27-1	34-53-2
Punts	4-48	4-40
Fumbles-Lost	1-1	3-1
Penalties-Yards	6-39	7-47
Time of Possession	32:26	27:34

INDIVIDUALS
AUBURN
Rushing
Player	Att.	Yds.	TD	Long
Bostic	19	183	3	41
Davis	11	73	0	16
Richardson	7	56	1	28
McMillon	3	3	0	2
Sanders	1	2	0	2
White	4	-14	0	0

Passing
Player	A-C-I	Yds	TD	Long
White	27-16-1	192	1	34

Receiving
Player	No.	Yds	TD	Long
Sanders	5	89	1	34
McMillon	3	41	0	26
Carder	3	26	0	14
Davis	2	9	0	10
Bailey	1	12	0	12
Bostic	1	4	0	4
Richardson	1	11	0	11

Punting
Player	No.	Yds	Avg	Long
Daniel	4	192	48.0	57

Returns
Player	Punts	Kickoff	Int.
Shelling		1-0	1-73
Johnson			1-0
Bailey	2-6	3-64	

GEORGIA
Rushing
Player	Att.	Yds.	TD	Long
Davis	11	73	1	37
Montgomery	11	20	0	15
Harvey	1	5	0	5
Fouch	1	0	0	0
Zeier	11	-16	0	13

Passing
Player	A-C-I	Yds	TD	Long
Zeier	53-34-2	426	3	76

Receiving
Player	No.	Yds	TD	Long
Graham	10	175	1	76
Hunter	10	84	1	23
Thomas	6	57	0	12
Bohannon	4	76	1	50
Mitchell	4	34	0	21

Punting
Player	No.	Yds	Avg	Long
Armstrong	4	160	40	52

Returns
Player	Punts	Kickoff	Int.
Thompson			1-7
McCranie	1-39	5-10	

DEFENSE
AUBURN
Tackles, assists — Mounds 4-0; Shelling 7-1; C.Jackson 10-0; Richardson 1-3; Solomon 2-3; Miska 3-3; Pelton 3-2; Harris 3-6; Primus 3-2; Whitehead 1-0; Johnson 0-0; McGee 2-0; Atkins 1-0; Miller 2-1; Walker 1-1; Hart 1-1.

Sacks — Pelton, Primus, Atkins, Miller, Walker, Hart Fumbles recovered — Jackson Passes intercepted — Shelling, Johnson. Passes broken up — Richardson 3, Harris, Whitehead 1.

GEORGIA
Tackles, assists — Owens 0-1; Wilson 3-3; Yancy 3-0; Thompson 2-2; Butler 0-2; Muschamp 2-4; Marshall 2-3; Godfrey 2-2; Pledger 0-1; Clemons 10-3; Davis 2-0; Smith 2-3; Rosenberg 1-1; Johnson 0-2; Daniels 0-7; Fouch 1-1; Jones 1-0

Sacks — Smith. Fumbles recovered — Marshall, Meadows. Passes intercepted — Thompson. Passes broken up — Yancy.

AUBURN SEASON
Results (10-0)

Sept. 2	Ole Miss,	Won 16-12
Sept. 11	Samford,	Won 35-7
Sept. 18	at LSU,	Won 34-10
Sept. 25	Southern Miss,	Won 35-24
Oct. 2	at Vandy,	Won 14-10
Oct. 9	Miss. State,	Won 31-17
Oct. 16	Florida,	Won 38-35
Oct. 30	at Arkansas,	Won 38-21
Nov. 6	New Mexico St.,	Won 55-14
Nov. 13	at Georgia,	Won 42-28
Nov. 20	Alabama	

Chapter Four

Auburn 1993 By The Numbers

1993 AUBURN TIGER ALPHABETICAL ROSTER

No.	Name	Pos.	Ht.	Wt.	Class	Exp.	Hometown (High School/JC)
64	Brian Adcock	OL	6-3	256	Fr.	RS	Tampa, Fla. (Chamberlain)
72	Russ Aldridge	DE	6-5	243	So.	RS	Columbus, Ga. (Shaw)
68	Shay Allen	OG	6-4	267	Fr.	RS	Prattville, Ala. (Prattville)
99	Ace Atkins	DE	6-4	213	Sr.	1L	Atlanta, Ga. (Auburn)
59	Toby Anderson	LB	5-8	213	So.	SQ	Eufaula, Ala. (Eufaula)
94	Torris Babbs	TE	6-2	254	So.	SQ	Talladega, Ala. (Talladega)
18	Thomas Bailey	WR	6-0	196	Jr.	2L	Enterprise, Ala. (Enterprise)
14	Allen Barnett	QB	6-2	202	Fr.	RS	Alexander City, Ala. (Benjamin Russell)
67	Bucky Beddingfield	OL	6-2	271	So.	SQ	Jackson, Ga. (Jackson)
52	Todd Boland	OT	6-3	257	Jr.	1L	New Brockton, Ala. (New Brockton)
33	James Bostic	TB	6-0	224	Jr.	2L	Ft. Lauderdale, Fla. (Dillard)
62	Brian Brinsfield	SN	6-1	201	Jr.	2L	Spanish Fort, Ala. (Fairhope)
21	James Bryan	FB	5-8	196	So.	1L	Tehachapi, Calif. (Tehachapi)
97	Myron Burton	DE	6-5	266	Fr.	RS	Columbus, Ga. (Shaw)
86	Sean Carder	WR	5-9	172	Sr.	1L	Marietta, Ga. (Marietta)
58	Wayne Cary	OG	6-1	256	Jr.	SQ	Huntsville, Ala. (Lee)
28	Pedro Cherry	WR	6-1	208	Sr.	3L	Windsor, N.C. (Bertie)
27	Sean Clarke	FS	6-0	191	So.	SQ	Birmingham, Ala. (Pelham)
92	Rahmon Cooper	DE	6-2	229	Fr.	RS	Birmingham, Ala. (Parker)
30	Kelsey Crook	DB	5-9	164	Jr.	SQ	Ohatchee, Ala. (Ohatchee)
36	Terry Daniel	P	6-1	226	Jr.	1L	Valley, Ala. (Valley)
83	Matt DeValk	TE	6-5	214	Fr.	HS	Daphne, Ala. (Daphne)
39	Sean Davidson	WR	5-7	186	Sr.	1L	Athens, Ala. (Elkmont)
51	Chris Dewberry	FB	5-10	196	Fr.	HS	Valley, Ala. (Valley)
49	Derrick Dorn	TE	6-4	211	So.	1L	Daleville, Ala. (Daleville)
37	Ben Efird	WR	5-8	149	Jr.	SQ	Birmingham, Ala. (Hewitt-Trussville)
47	Pat Epkins	LB	6-1	201	Fr.	RS	Prattville, Ala. (Prattville)
91	Alonzo Etheridge	DE	6-4	255	Jr.	2L	Selma, Ala. (Selma)
13	Scott Etheridge	PK	5-11	148	Sr.	1L	Valencia, Calif. (Hart)
35	Demond Fields	TE	6-0	229	Fr.	RS	Spartanburg, S.C. (Spartanburg)
75	John Franklin	OT	6-9	252	Fr.	RS	Graceville, Fla. (Graceville)
5	Joe Frazier	TB	6-0	212	Jr.	2L	Montgomery, Ala. (Lanier)
82	Andy Fuller	TE	6-3	243	So.	1L	Huntsville, Ala. (Johnson)
74	Wayne Gandy	OT	6-5	275	Sr.	3L	Haines City, Fla. (Haines City)
16	Thery George	P	6-2	194	Jr.	1L	Seale, Ala. (Woodland Christian)
53	Anthony Harris	LB	6-2	221	So.	1L	Ft. Pierce, Fla. (Westwood)
98	Randy Hart	DT	6-5	287	Sr.	2L	Enterprise, Ala. (Enterprise)
9	Clay Helton	QB	6-2	205	Jr.	1L	Palos Verdi, Calif. (Clements)
63	Chris Holland	OL	6-5	263	So.	1L	Pensacola, Fla. (Pensacola)
8	Calvin Jackson	CB	5-10	179	So.	1L	Ft. Lauderdale, Fla. (Dillard)
15	Marc Johnson	FS	6-1	190	Sr.	3L	Centre, Ala. (Cherokee County)
42	Bryan Karkoska	PK	5-10	194	Sr.	1L	Tallahassee, Fla. (Leon)
46	John Kolen	LB	6-0	200	Fr.	RS	Montgomery, Ala. (Trinity)
93	Ramon Luster	DT	6-2	279	So.	SQ	Birmingham, Ala. (Ensley)
29	Roymon Malcolm	TB	6-3	222	So.	SQ	Ruston, La. (Ruston)
80	Shaun Malone	TE	6-6	240	So.	1L	Madison, Ala. (Bob Jones)
24	Dell McGee	WR	5-8	181	So.	1L	Columbus, Ga. (Kendrick)
41	Reid McMilion	FB	6-0	221	Sr.	3L	Selma, Ala. (Morgan Academy)
38	David Milford	FS	6-2	192	Sr.	1L	Birmingham, Ala. (South Mecklenburg)
95	Andre Miller	DE	6-2	246	So.	1L	Meridian, Miss. (Meridian)
45	Jason Miska	LB	6-2	202	So.	SQ	Bridgeport, Conn.
12	Harold Morrow	TB	6-0	198	So.	1L	Maplesville, Ala. (Maplesville)
2	Otis Mounds	FS	6-0	194	Jr.	2L	Ft. Lauderdale, Fla. (Dillard)
10	Patrick Nix	QB	6-2	188	So.	1L	Rainbow City, Ala. (Etowah)
78	Brian Osborn	OT	6-5	293	Jr.	1L	Plant City, Fla. (Plant City)
50	Mike Pelton	LB	6-3	262	Jr.	2L	Goshen, Ala. (Goshen)
23	Michael Pina	CB	6-1	196	Sr.	3L	Merritt Island, Fla. (Merritt Island)
77	Damon Primus	DT	6-3	278	Jr.	1L	Detroit, Mich. (M.L. King)
65	Anthony Redmond	OG	6-5	288	Sr.	3L	Brewton, Ala. (T.R. Miller)
61	Eric Reebals	LB	5-11	192	Fr.	HS	Homewood, Ala. (Homewood)
22	Adrian Reese	TB	6-0	197	Fr.	RS	Auburn, Ala. (Auburn)
40	Tony Richardson	FB	6-2	219	Sr.	3L	Daleville, Ala. (Daleville)
25	Darryl Riggins	CB	6-1	182	Fr.	RS	Ft. Pierce, Fla. (Central)
20	Brian Robinson	SS	6-3	194	So.	1L	Ft. Lauderdale, Fla. (Dillard)
73	Jim Roe	OT	6-5	281	Fr.	RS	Mauldin, S.C. (Mauldin)
31	Charles Rose	WR	5-11	177	So.	1L	Leeds, Ala. (Leeds)
56	Shannon Roubique	OG	6-1	278	So.	1L	Denham Springs, La. (Denham Springs)
70	Daryl Sanders	OT	6-3	306	Fr.	RS	Roanoke, Ala. (Handley)
81	Frank Sanders	WR	6-2	200	Jr.	2L	Ft. Lauderdale, Fla. (Dillard)
48	Robert Scott	WR	5-10	160	So.	1L	Winter Haven, Fla. (Winter Haven)
4	Chris Shelling	SS	5-10	180	Jr.	2L	Columbus, Ga. (Baker)
6	Fred Smith	CB	5-9	190	Jr.	2L	Eufaula, Ala. (Eufaula)
85	Les Snead	TE	6-0	235	Sr.	TR	Eufaula, Ala. (Eufaula)
44	Terry Solomon	LB	6-2	224	So.	1L	Cairo, Ga. (Cairo)
71	Matt Stone	OL	6-1	248	Fr.	RS	Birmingham, Ala. (Berry)
17	Patrick Sullivan	QB	6-3	200	Fr.	RS	Birmingham, Ala. (Mountain Brook)
66	Jason Taylor	OG	6-1	295	So.	1L	Mobile, Ala. (Shaw)
60	Leonard Thomas	OG	6-2	270	Fr.	RS	Columbus, Ga. (Kendrick)
54	Greg Thompson	C	6-2	252	Sr.	3L	Enterprise, Ala. (Enterprise)
55	Carlos Thornton	LB	6-1	233	Jr.	2L	Paceli, Ala. (Holy Trinity)
84	Otis Thornton	WR	6-5	180	Jr.	SQ	Birmingham, Ala. (Ensley)
96	Gary Walker	DE	6-3	258	Jr.	TR	Lavonia, Ga. [Hinds (Miss.) JC]
76	Ricardo Walker	DT	6-2	275	Fr.	RS	Darlington, S.C. (St. John's)
11	Stan White	QB	6-3	202	Sr.	3L	Birmingham, Ala. (Berry)
90	Willie Whitehead	DE	6-3	231	Jr.	2L	Tuskegee, Ala. (Tuskegee)
13	Jamie Williams	QB	5-11	187	Fr.	RS	Union Springs, Ala. (Bullock Memorial)
32	Ted Yarbrough	TB	5-10	201	So.	1L	Blakely, Ga. (Early County)

1993 AUBURN UNIVERSITY FOOTBALL SUPERLATIVES

Individual

LONGEST RUN FROM SCRIMMAGE:	64, McMilion vs. Southern Miss (9-25)
LONGEST PASS FROM SCRIMMAGE:	57, White-Sanders vs. LSU (9-18)
LONGEST PUNT RETURN:	30, Carder vs. Samford (9-11), Bailey vs. Alabama (11-20)
LONGEST INTERCEPTION RETURN:	96, Jackson vs. Florida (10-16)
LONGEST KICKOFF RETURN:	31, Bailey vs. Florida (10-16)
MOST RUSHING ATTEMPTS:	28, Bostic vs. Ole Miss (9-2)
MOST YARDS RUSHING:	183, Bostic vs. Georgia (11-13)
MOST TOUCHDOWNS RUSHING:	3, Bostic vs. Southern Miss (9-25) and Georgia (11-13)
MOST PASSES ATTEMPTED:	35, White vs. Florida (10-16)
MOST PASSES COMPLETED:	23, White vs. Florida (10-16) and New Mexico State
MOST YARDS PASSING:	282: White vs. LSU (9-18)
MOST PASS RECEPTIONS:	7 (134) Sanders vs. Arkansas (10-30)
MOST TOUCHDOWN PASSES THROWN:	3, White vs. Samford (9-11) and New Mexico State
MOST YARDS RECEIVING:	134 (7 rec), Sanders vs. Arkansas (10-30)
MOST TOTAL YARDS:	299 (282 passing, 17 rushing), White vs. LSU
MOST POINTS SCORED:	18, Bostic vs. Southern Miss (9-25) and Georgia (11-13)
MOST POINTS SCORED KICKING:	12, S. Etheridge vs. New Mexico State (10-6)
MOST INTERCEPTIONS:	1, Harris, Robinson, Jackson, Shelling, Johnson, McGee
MOST PUNTS:	7, Daniel vs. Ole Miss (9-2) and Alabama (11-20)
BEST PUNTING AVERAGE:	52.4, Daniel vs. Florida (10-16)
LONGEST PUNT:	71, Daniel vs. Florida (10-15)
LONGEST FIELD GOAL:	41, Etheridge vs. Florida (10-16)

HIGH AND LOW

Team

OFFENSE	BEST	WORST
POINTS SCORED	55 vs. NMS	16 vs. UM
FIRST DOWNS	31 vs. NMS	16 vs. UM
By Rushing	15 vs. LSU, NMS	8 vs. UF
By Passing	15 vs. NMS	5 vs. UM, UA
By Penalty	3 vs. UA	0 vs. AR, UG
RUSHING YARDS	303 vs. Ug	180 vs. SU
Passing Yards	290 vs. NMS	79 vs. UM
TOTAL NET YARDS	579 vs. NMS	272 vs. UM
TOTAL PLAYS	86 vs. NMS	60 vs. SU
By Rushing	56 vs. UM, USM	45 vs. SU
By Passing	40 vs. NMS	15 vs. SU
PASSES COMPLETED	23 vs. UF, NMS	8 vs. UM
PASSES HAD INTERCEPTED	0 vs. SU, UF	1 vs. UM, LSU, USM, AR, UA
FUMBLES LOST	0 vs. UF	4 vs. LSU
YARDS PENALIZED	37 vs. UA	110 vs. LSU
PUNTS	2 vs. AR	7 vs. UM, UA

DEFENSE	BEST	WORST
FIRSST DOWNS ALLOWED	8 vs. UM, NMS	10 vs. UG
By Rushing	2 vs. MNS	10 vs. UG
By Passing	4 vs. USM	16 vs. UG
By Penalty	0 vs. USM	2 vs. UF
RUSHING YARDS ALLOWED	47 vs. UM	174 vs. UF
PASSING YARDS ALLOWED	103 vs. LSU	426 vs. UG
TOTAL NET YARDS ALLOWED	176 vs. UM	560 vs. UF
TOTAL PLAYS ALLOWED	46 vs. UM	88 vs. UG
By Rushing	24 vs. NMS	45 vs. SU
By Passing	15 vs. SU	53 vs. UG
PASS COMPLETIONS ALLOWED	8 vs. UF, UG, UA	34 vs. UG
PASSES INTERCEPTED	2 vs. UF, UG, UA	0 vs. SU
FUMBLES RECOVERED	2 vs. USM	0 vs. NMS, UA
TOTAL TURNOVERS	3 vs. SU, USM, UF, UG	2 vs. UM, LSU, AR, UA
PUNTS FORCED	10 vs. UM, LSU	4 vs. UG

1993 AUBURN DEFENSIVE STATISTICS*

(Through Alabama Game)

Player, Position	Total	Solo-Asst	Tl-Yds	SKS-Yds	CF	RF	PBU	INT-Yds
Jason, Miska, LB	125	68-57	4-6	2-9	0	0	4	0
Anthony Harris, LB	123	53-70	8-17	7-32	0	1	10	1-4
Terry Solomon, LB	77	42-35	1-1	0-0	4	0	7	5-131
Brian Robinson, FS	74	43-31	1-1	0-0	4	0	7	5-131
Chris Shelling, CB	74	46-28	2-14	0-0	1	0	6	4-169
Mike Pelton, DT	73	42-31	9-26	5-36	1	2	0	0
Damon Primus, DT	72	43-29	9-30	5-16	1	0	0	0
Randy Hart, DT	69	34-35	3-10	5-19	0	0	0	0
Willie Whitehead, DE	63	31-32	6-33	3-13	0	0	3	0
Otis Mounds, SS	61	32-29	2-6	0-0	0	0	4	1-15
Gary Walker, DE	61-	38-23	6-19	5-26	0	2	4	0
Calvin Jackson, CB	52	38-14	0-0	0-0	0	1	18	2-104
Alonzo Etheridge, DE	27	17-10	2-3	030	0	0	0	0
Andre Miller, DE	23	7-16	0-0	2-8	2	0	1	0
Derrick Robinson, LB	19	7-12	0-0	0-0	0	1	0	0
Dell McGee, CB	16	13-3	0-0	0-0	0	0	2	1-0
Marcellus Mostella, LB	13	5-8	1-1	0-0	0	1	4	0
Mike Pina, CB	12	5-7	0-0	0-0	0	0	0	0
Ace Atkins, DE	11	5-6	0-0	3-22	0	0	0	0
Kelsey Crook, CB	11	8-3	0-0	0-0	0	2	0	0
Joe Frazier, LB	11	7-4	0-0	0-0	0	0	0	0
Carlos Thornton, LB	11	9-2	0-0	0-0	1	0	0	0
Ramon Luster, DT	8	4-4	0-0	1-8	0	0	1	0
Marc Johnson, FS	7	2-5	0-0	0-0	0	0	0	1-0
Harold Morrow, RB	6	3-3	0-0	0-0	0	0	0	0
Roymon Malcom, TB	5	3-2	0-0	0-0	0	0	0	0
James Bryan, TB	3	3-0	0-0	0-0	0	0	0	0
Ricardo Walker, DT	3	2-1	0-0	0-0	0	0	0	0
Terry Daniel, P	2	2-0	0-0	0-0	0	0	0	0
Tohy Anderson, LB	1	1-0	0-0	0-0	0	0	0	0
James Bostic , TB	1	1-0	0-0	0-0	0	0	0	0
Myron Burton, DE	1	1-0	0-0	0-0	0	0	0	0
Sean Clarke, CB	1	1-0	0-0	0-0	0	0	0	0
Scott Etheridge, PK	1	1-0	0-0	0-0	0	0	0	0
Wayne Gandy, OT	1	1-0	0-0	0-0	0	0	0	0
Tony Richardson, FB	1	1-0	0-0	0-0	1	0	0	0
Jamie Williams, CB	1	0-1	0-0	0-0	0	0	0	0

TL-Tackle For Loss SKS-Sacks CF-Caused Fumble RF-Recovered Fumble PBU-Pass Broken Up INT-Interception

*Taken from game film

1993 GAME STATISTICS

PASSING

PLAYER	*G*	*ATT*	*CMP*	*INT*	*PCT*	*YDS*	*YDS/G*	*RTNG*	*TD*	*LP*
White, Stan	11	271	164	8	.605	2057	187.0	134.2	13	57
Nix, Patrick	5	15	10	0	.667	131	26.2	184.0	2	35
Sanders, Frank	11	1	0	0	.000	0	0.0	0.0	0	0
Sullivan, Patrick	3	1	0	0	.000	0	0.0	0.0	0	0
AUBURN	11	288	174	8	.604	2188	198.9	135.9	15	57
Opponent	11	349	153	15	.438	2039	185.4	98.5	15	

RECEIVING

PLAYER	*G*	*REC*	*YDS*	*AVG*	*RPG*	*TD*	*LP*
Sanders, Frank	11	48	842	17.5	4.4	6	57
Richardson, Tony	11	28	273	9.8	2.5	2	23
Bailey, Thomas	11	27	427	15.8	2.5	4	57
Dorn, Derrick	11	12	122	10.2	1.1	0	23
McMilion, Reid	11	12	94	7.8	1.1	0	26
Davis, Stephen	9	11	122	11.1	1.2	1	35
Carder, Sean	11	11	111	10.1	1.0	0	17
Bostic, James	11	10	40	4.0	0.9	1	19
Morrow, Harold	9	5	41	8.2	0.6	0	20
Fuller, Andy	10	2	26	13.0	0.2	0	19
Gosha, Willie	11	2	19	9.5	0.2	0	12
Malcolm, Raymon	10	2	17	8.5	0.2	1	11
Goodson, Tyrone	1	1	32	32.0	1.0	0	32
McCovery, Jesse	11	1	9	9.0	0.1	0	9
Davidson, Sean	10	1	8	8.0	0.1	0	5
Battle, Lewis	8	1	5	5.0	0.1	0	5
AUBURN	11	174	2188	12.6	15.8	15	57
Opponent	11	153	2039	13.3	13.9	15	

INTERCEPTIONS

PLAYER	*G*	*NO*	*YDS*	*AVG*	*TD*	*LP*
Robinson, Brian	11	5	131	26.2	2	45
Shelling, Chris	11	4	169	42.3	1	73
Jackson, Calvin	11	2	104	52.0	1	96
Mounds, Otis	10	1	15	15.0	0	15
Harris, Anthony	11	1	4	4.0	0	4
McGee, Dell	11	1	0	0.0	0	0
Johnson, Marc	11	1	0	0.0	0	0
AUBURN	11	15	423	28.2	4	96
Opponents	11	8	49	6.1	1	

continued—

SCORING

PLAYER	TD	2PT	XP	DXP	SAF	FG	PTS
Etheridge	0	0- 0	45-45	0- 0	0	12-15	81
Bostic, J	13	0- 0	0- 0	0- 0	0	0- 0	78
Sandera, F	7	0- 0	0- 0	0- 0	0	0- 0	42
Richardson	6	0- 0	0- 0	0- 0	0	0- 0	36
Davis, S	4	0- 0	0- 0	0- 0	0	0- 0	24
Bailey, T	4	0- 0	0- 0	0- 0	0	0- 0	24
White, S	4	0- 0	0- 0	0- 0	0	0- 0	24
Malcolm, R	2	0- 0	0- 0	0- 0	0	0- 0	12
McMilion	1	0- 0	0- 0	0- 0	0	0- 0	6
Jackson, C	1	0- 0	0- 0	0- 0	0	0- 0	6
Shelling,	1	0- 0	0- 0	0- 0	0	0- 0	6
AUBURN	45	0- 0	45-45	0- 0	1	12-15	353
Opponents	24	2- 4	20-20	0- 0	0	8-13	192

SCORING BY QUARTERS			*1ST*	*2ND*	*3RD*	*4TH*		*TOT*
AUBURN		65	131	86	71	353	32.1	
Opponent		51	48	44	49	192	17.5	

PUNTING

PLAYER	6	MO	YDS	AVG	LP	BLK
Daniel, Terry	11	51	2393	46.9	71	0
AUBURN	11	51	2393	46.6	71	0
Opponents	11	73	2921	40.0		0

KICKOFF RETURNS

PLAYER	G	MO	YDS	AVG	TD	LP
Bailey, Thomas	11	26	504	19.4	0	31
Davis, Stephen	9	1	25	25.0	0	25
McCovery, Jesse	11	1	8	8.0	0	8
Carder, Sean	11	1	0	0.0	0	0
McMilion, Reid	11	1	0	0.0	0	0
Shelling, Chris	11	1	0	0.0	0	0
AUBURN	11	31	537	17.3	0	31
Opponent	11	40	889	22.2	0	

continued—

PUNT RETURNS

PLAYER	G	MO	YDS	AVG	TD	LP
Bailey, Thomas	11	27	210	7.8	0	30
Carder, Sean	11	2	37	18.5	0	30
Battle, Lewis	8	3	17	5.7	0	9
Shelling, Chris	11	1	0	0.0	0	0
AUBURN	11	33	264	8.0	0	30
Opponents	11	26	418	16.1	1	

MISCELLANEOUS YARDS (Fumbles Advanced)

PLAYER	G	ATT	YDS	AVG	PG	TD
Jackson, Calvin	11	1	1	1.0	0.1	0
AUBURN	11	1	1	1.0	0.1	0
Opponents	11	2	12	6.0	1.1	0

FIELD GOAL ACCURACY	-20	20-29	30-39	40-49	50+
Etheridge, Scott	0-0	7-7	4-5	1-3	0-0 12-15
AUBURN	0-0	7-7	4-5	1-3	0-0 12-15

FIELD GOAL DISTANCES

Etheridge, Scott   Made: 27,37,29,24,36,32,41,37,27,26,23,26

                     Missed: 43,35,40

THIRD DOWN CONVERSIONS BY QUARTERS

	1st	2nd	3rd	4th	Total	Pct.
AUBURN	11-33	11-34	20-41	15-38	57-146	.390
Opponents	11-39	10-42	9-30	13-46	43-157	.274

FOURTH DOWN CONVERSIONS BY QUARTERS

	1st	2nd	3rd	4th	Total	Pct.
AUBURN	0-0	1-1	1-3	2-6	4-10	.400
Opponents	1-1	1-2	1-2	4-15	7-20	.350

1993 ATTENDANCE FIGURES:

	Totals	Average
Home:	567,436	81,062
Road:	247,997	61,999

1993 AUBURN FOOTBALL STATISTICS
"FINAL 11 GAME TOTALS"

OVERALL RECORD: 11-0-0 SEC: 8-0-0 HOME: 7-0-0 ROAD: 4-0-0

1993 GAME RESULTS

DATE	OPPONENT	ATT.	SCORE
09-02	Ole Miss	78, 246	16-12
09-11	Samford	68, 936	35-7
09-18	LSU	71, 936	34-10
09-25	Southern Mississippi	83, 476	35-24
10-02	Vanderbilt	40, 527	14-10
10-09	Mississippi State	84, 222	31-17
10-16	Florida	85, 214	38-35
10-30	Arkansas	50, 100	31-21
11-06	New Mexico State	82, 128	55-14
11-13	Georgia	85, 434	42-28
11-20	Alabama	85, 214	22-14

TEAM STATISTICS	AUBURN	OPP
Total First Downs	248	166
First Downs-Rushing	133	72
First Downs-Passing	99	82
First Downs Penalty	16	12
Fumbles/Lost	23-14	17-10
Penalties/Yards	66-551	69-639
Sacks by/Yds. Lost	24-141	18-125
Third Down Conversions	57-146	43-157
Third Down Conversion Pct.	.390	.274
Fourth Down Conversions	4-10	7-20
Fourth Down Conversion Pct.	.400	.350
Avg. Time of Possession	33:49	26:11

TOTAL OFFENSE

PLAYER	G	PLAY	RUSH	PASS	TOTAL	AVG
White, Stan	11	350	33	2057	2090	190.0
Bostic, James	11	199	1205	0	1205	109.6
Davis, Stephen	9	87	480	0	480	53.3
Richardson, Tony	11	58	249	0	249	22.6
Nix, Patrick	5	20	-19	131	112	22.4
McMillion, Reid	11	38	232	0	232	21.1
Maclcolm, Raymon	10	15	113	0	113	11.3
Morrow, Harold	9	13	49	0	49	5.4
Sanders, Frank	11	7	57	0	57	5.2
Sullivan, Patrick	3	3	10	0	10	3.3
Bryan, James	7	5	18	0	18	2.6
Frazier, Joe	11	4	21	0	21	1.9
Carder Sean	11	2	-16	0	-16	-1.5
AUBURN	11	800	2432	2188	4620	420.0
Opponent	11	698	1406	2039	3445	313.2

RUSHING

PLAYER	G	ATT	GAIN	LOST	YDS	AVG	PG
Bostic, James	11	199	1254	49	1205	6.1	109.6
Davis, Stephen	9	87	496	16	480	5.5	53.3
Richardson, Tony	11	58	250	1	249	4.3	22.6
McMilion, Reid	11	38	234	2	232	6.1	21.1
Malcolm, Royman	10	15	113	0	113	7.5	11.5
Sanders, Frank	11	6	57	0	57	9.5	5.2
Morrow, Harold	9	13	50	1	49	3.8	5.4
White, Stan	11	79	208	175	33	0.4	3.0
Frazier, Joe	11	4	21	0	21	5.3	1.9
Bryan, James	7	5	19	1	18	3.6	2.6
Sullivan, Patrick	3	2	10	0	10	5.0	3.3
Carder, Sean	11	2	0	16	-16	-8.0	-1.5
Nix, Patrick	5	5	2	21	-19	-3.8	-3.8
AUBURN	11	513	2714	282	2432	4.7	221.1
Opponents	11	350	1686	280	1406	4.0	127.8

Auburn quarterback Stan White, returning to greatness in a season to erase frustrations of the past.

1993 AUBURN FOOTBALL SCHEDULE

DATE	OPPONENT	SITE	TIME	SCORE
Sept. 2	Ole Miss	AUBURN	7:00	16-12
Sept. 11	Samford	AUBURN	6:00	35-7
Sept. 18	LSU	Baton Rouge	7:00	34-10
Sept. 25	Southern Miss	AUBURN	1:00	35-24
Oct. 2	Vanderbilt	Nashville	7:00	14-10
Oct. 9	Miss. State	AUBURN	1:00	31-17
Oct. 16	Florida	AUBURN	1:00	38-35
Oct. 30	Arkansas	Fayetteville	2:00	31-21
Nov. 6	New Mexico St.	AUBURN	1:00	55-14
Nov. 13	Georgia	Athens	12:00	42-28
Nov. 20	Alabama	AUBURN	1:00	22-14

Wayne Gandy celebrates a perfect season as he parades the field with an Auburn banner after the Alabama game
Steve Barnette photo

*The heat of battle shows on Willie Anderson's face as he gets a breather during the Auburn-
Alabama game*
Steve Barnette photo

Primus (77) and Hart (98) share the joy of their victory over Alabama and an 11-0 season
Steve Barnette photo

A word of thanks

Instant books take lots of people doing everything just right, and The Birmingham News is blessed with people who not only do things right, but do them fast, with skill, talent and good humor.

I want to thank those people who went the extra mile to put this book together during Thanksgiving week, already one of the busiest weeks of the year.

News librarian Ann Hobbs and state editor Glenn Stephens, who gave up their Sunday after the Auburn-Alabama game to transfer all of the stories out of electronic archives.

Charles Nesbitt, spent much of Saturday night, Sunday and Sunday night after the game pulling together and making prints of every picture that you see in this book.

News sports editor Wayne Hester, not only for guiding Auburn football coverage throughout the season, but for writing a foreword to this book and making sure stories were where they needed to be when they needed to be there.

Auburn beat reporter Neal Sims. I cannot remember when, week in and week out, that writing quality throughout a season was so good.

Charles Burttram, Alicia Archibald and Andrea Kantargis, who dropped what they were doing to give the book a final proofing.

Michelle Segrest, who keyboarded and proofed stories that had been written before *The News* had an electronic archive system.

Designer Lori Smith, who always comes through, even when it means missing a few nights sleep.

Tommy Russell and Lamar Gregory and all of LaJune Mitchell's folks who do all those mechanical things behind the scenes that actually make things happen.

The News color lab--especially Al Pardue--who handled all the color separations overnight. I'm sure I missed someone. The gratitude is there, I want you to know.

One tidbit: Auburn folks always are talking about the "Auburn family." You might be interested to know that beat writer Neal Sims, writer and proofreader Michelle Segrest and designer Lori Smith all graduated from Auburn.

So, here's to you, Auburn faithful. I hope you enjoy memories of this wonderful season for many years, and I hope that in its way our book will help you keep those memories alive.

Tom Bailey
Director of Special Projects
The Birmingham News